OFF THE BEATEN PATH

Short Hikes in the White Mountains

by

John Henderson

Photographs by John Henderson
Graphics by Don Wallace Studio

Glen-Bartlett Publishing Company
Westboro, Massachusetts 1979

Library of Congress Catalog Card Number: 79-51803
ISBN: 0-9602802-0-0

Cover Photo: Mount Osceola from Snows Mountain

Printed in the USA by
Whitman Press, Inc., Lebanon, NH

To Joan, Scott, and Elise
Hiking Companions, Supportive Throughout

Carter Notch from Pine Mountain

Acknowledgements

This Guide is the product of long hours and the efforts of many people. I thank you all. Special thanks to Joanne Clancy, Anita Drujon, David Meyers, and Linda Skinner.

Several quotations have been reprinted from the White Mountain Guide, courtesy of the Appalachian Mountain Club.

Map Legends

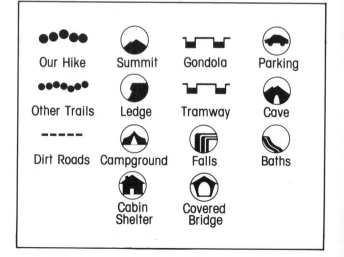

CONTENTS

MAP OF THE AREA

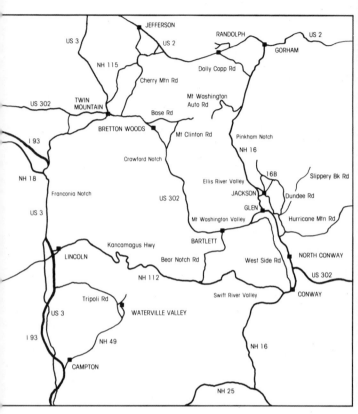

The White Mountains of New Hampshire

INTRODUCTION

The White Mountains

The White Mountains of New Hampshire are unique. They form the largest mountain mass east of the Mississippi River and north of the Carolinas. Their character changes with the seasons, the days, and, seemingly, with the wind. Relatively small for mountains (the highest peak is Mount Washington at 6288 feet in elevation), they combine two properties making them unique: dense forests at the lower elevations and bare, rocky expanses at the higher elevations. Hundreds of miles of foot paths have been cut through the mountains, yet many visitors to the area fail to explore these trails.

A number of guides to the region exist, the most extensive being the Appalachian Mountain Club White Mountain Guide. The emphasis of these guides is, primarily, on the already overcrowded trails of the Franconia and the Presidential Ranges, and on the conquest of the higher peaks—the 4000-footers. Very little is written about the shorter trails in the White Mountains.

The Purpose of this Guide

The purpose of this guide is to encourage families with small children to discover the pleasure of walking within the White Mountains. The emphasis is on short hikes at the lower elevations—no hike longer than four hours and none above an elevation of 3400 feet. No matter how young your trampers or where you are staying within the White Mountains, you will find walks for your family in this guide.

You don't need special gear. To lessen erosion of the trails, people climb even the most difficult mountains in tennis shoes. However, a day pack is good to have for sweaters and snacks.

A summary page for every hike precedes the description of the trail. There is a map of each trail, detailing landmarks and outlooks. The trail descriptions are SUBJECTIVE, giving a personal recollection of our family's experiences. On occasion, an historical sketch gives insight into this region, rich in its Indian heritage.

During the summer of 1977, we hiked all of these trails with our two children who were four and eight years old. The trail descriptions are from our experience. Some of the trails we hiked more than once; some we hiked with other families and friends. The weather conditions varied from very warm to quite cool, from cloudy to cloudless, and from dry to pouring rain.

The Summary Page

The summary has five categories: a general description of the trail, trail statistics, a summary of our experience, directions for finding the trail, and a trail map.

General Trail Description. The general trail description is a short summary of the hike, its goal, and its return (whether a loop, a distinct return path to a point near the start of the trail, or back along the same path). When hiking with children, having a goal makes the walk more exciting. The goal might be a waterfall, a ledge with an open outlook, or just a pleasant clearing for a picnic.

Trail Statistics. The trail statistics come from the US Geological Survey maps of the area and the AMC White Mountain Guide. I have tried hard for accuracy but cannot guarantee every figure. The statistics include:

the starting elevation of the trail

the maximum elevation along the trail

the total vertical climbed

the total distance traveled

the nature of any blazes that mark the trail

the availability of drinking water along the trail.

Our Experience. Difficulty was rated, as much as possible, from the perspective of our younger child.

Our pace was NOT NECESSARILY related to difficulty. Obviously, we negotiated difficult trails at a slow pace, but sometimes we maintained a slow pace over easy trails to enjoy the day, the views, the woods.

Enjoyment was influenced by many factors—the weather, trail conditions, and our mood. When late in the summer our son woke to say, "Good. It's raining. Dad won't want to hike today.", we knew we were off to a bad start. If the hike was fair to us, don't let this deter you. Your experience will be different.

The recorded times, naturally, reflect our pace. Although times will vary considerably among different groups, ours can give you a RELATIVE idea of how long the hike is. Our times are generally long. We spend inordinate amounts of time along the trails while our children examine the undersides of ferns, feel the bark of trees, and attempt to catch every toad that crosses their paths. Plan to let the small ones mosey along and they'll be more likely to want to accompany you on your next walk.

The total hiking time serves as the basis for the organization of the guide, which is ordered from the shortest hike to the longest. The times do not include stops. Allow yourselves extra time to stop and enjoy the pleasures of the hike.

Directions to the Trail. The directions to the trail, used in conjunction with the map of the major arteries in the area, will enable you to find the trail without too much hunting and searching.

Please Help

I intend to expand this guide and to update it for accuracy. Please help. If you find inaccuracies or omissions, let me know by writing to:

Glen-Bartlett Publishing Company
105 West Main Street
Westboro, MA 01581.

The mountains seem unchanging, but the footpaths and man-made landmarks are not.

If this book leads a single family away from the mechanized attractions of the area to the woods and mountains, it will have served its purpose.

GLEN ELLIS FALLS

General Trail Description

Glen Ellis Falls are within a White Mountain National Forest Scenic Area. There is a wide, stone path leading down to the falls.

Trail Statistics

Starting Elevation	1950'
Ending Elevation	1875'
Total Vertical	75'
Total Distance	0.2 Mile
Blazes	None
Water	Yes

Our Experience

Difficulty	Very Easy
Our Pace	Slow
Enjoyment	Good

Time and Distance	Hours	Miles
NH 16 to the Falls	:10	0.1
Falls to NH 16	:10	0.1
Total	:20	0.2

Directions to the Trail

The Glen Ellis Falls Scenic Area parking is located on the west side of NH 16, 9 miles north of the covered bridge in Jackson and 0.3 mile south of the AMC Pinkham Notch Camp.

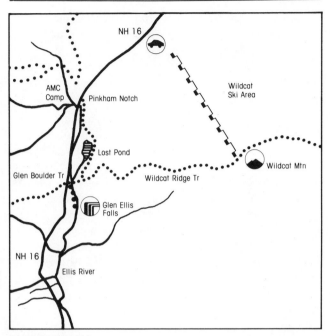

GLEN ELLIS FALLS

GLEN ELLIS FALLS

Scenic Areas have some bad vibrations associated with them—sights for the tourists who don't know where to look. However, we have found Glen Ellis Falls a pleasant and picturesque place to visit. The descriptive information on signs along the path gives a glimpse into the geological history of the falls and the surrounding valley.

The Ellis River. The Ellis River originates not far from the falls. Various streams, formed from melting snow and rainwater, flow down the eastern slopes of Mount Washington to form the river. It flows south through the Ellis River Valley and joins the Saco River in Glen. The Saco, which originates in Crawford Notch to the west, flows onward, through Maine, to the Atlantic.

At the Glen Ellis site the Ellis River flows along the east side of NH 16. A tunnel under the road leads from the parking area to the other side of the highway and the banks of the river. Following a stone path, we came to the head of the falls and an outlook to our left. We continued down a series of stairs to the foot of the falls.

The Falls. The water plunges over 60 feet. Hundreds of gallons a second flow into the deep, cold pool below. If you're brave, strip to your shorts and jump into the pool. There are no strictures against swimming here and, on a whim, many seem to take the plunge. If not that adventurous, just scramble out on the rocks and be cooled by the spray from the rushing cascade.

The valleys and cirques were formed 30,000 years ago when glaciers covered the entire state and slowly ground their way south. The ice, like a huge sheet of sandpaper, smoothed the mountain faces, carved the valleys, and carried rock and soil further south. The cirque of Glen Ellis was created when a series of avalanches from the eastern face of Wildcat Mountain carved the huge ravine by the sheer force of the rock slides. The water, having no choice, plunged then, as now, forward down the headwall into the ravine below.

This is an easy walk for even the youngest toddler. Glen Ellis is one of the most impressive falls in the White Mountains, and, also, one of the most accessible.

Maple Leaves

General Trail Description

This hike leads along the beginning of the Crawford Path to the Gibbs Falls along the Gibbs Brook. The return is by the same route.

Trail Statistics

Starting Elevation	1900'
Maximum Elevation	2100'
Total Vertical	200'
Total Distance	0.8 Mile
Blazes	None
Water	Yes

Our Experience

Difficulty	Easy
Our Pace	Moderate
Enjoyment	Fair

Time and Distance	Hours	Miles
US 302 to the Falls	:20	0.4
Falls to US 302	:15	0.4
Total	:35	0.8

Directions to the Trail

The Crawford Path leaves US 302, 2.9 miles north of the Willey House site. It lies just north of the Crawford Depot and just south of the junction with Mount Clinton Road that leaves east toward Marshfield Base Station. At the former site of the Crawford House, on both sides of the road, are parking areas. Park at either one; the trail for Gibbs Falls leaves on the Crawford Path just south of these areas along the east side of US 302.

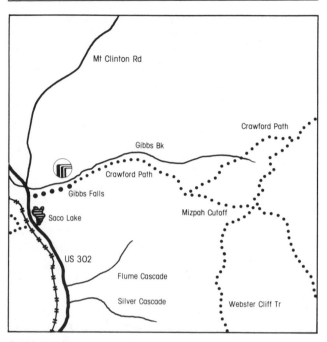

GIBBS FALLS

GIBBS FALLS

Gibbs Falls are reached by traveling less than a half-mile along the start of the Crawford Path. The Crawford Path was one of the many landmarks in the area of Crawford Notch in the early 1800's. A sign at the beginning of the path gives some history of the trail.

The Crawford Path. Crawford Path is the oldest, continuously-used mountain trail in America. The original path was cleared to Mount Clinton by Abel Crawford and his son, Ethan Allen, in 1819. The path was extended to Mount Washington and made a bridle path in 1840 by another of Abel's sons, Thomas. Abel had the distinction of being the first person to ascend Mount Washington on horseback using the Crawford Path. The trail is more than eight miles in length, over five of which are above the tree line. The section above the tree line gives some of the finest views in all of the White Mountains. It passes near the summits of the entire southern Presidential Range from Clinton, to Eisenhower, to Monroe, to Washington.

The Crawford Path begins away from, but quickly approaches, the south bank of Gibbs Brook. The path is wide and graded. It was easy for us to visualize horses beginning an ascent of Mount Washington. The trail begins a gentle, but deliberate, ascent.

Crawford Cliff. Within ten minutes, we came to a sign, **CRAWFORD CLIFF,** indicating a side trail left across Gibbs Brook. We decided to explore this trail and discover Crawford Cliff. Our report—don't bother. We climbed this side trail for 25 minutes until we came to a small outlook below a sheer rock cliff. Not believing this was the "cliff", we continued onward over a rough, barely-traveled trail up, up into the woods. Coming to nothing but rougher traveling, we finally returned to the outlook having decided it must be Crawford Cliff. There were good views of the Saco River, the Ammonoosuc Lakes, the Crawford House (which burned to the ground in the fall of 1977), and Mountains Field and Tom. We might have stayed, but we excited some bees who greatly excited us. We returned quickly to the side trail junction with Crawford Path.

The path continues its rise, and, within 20 minutes, comes to a sign on the left, GIBBS FALLS. Take the side path left leading down a steep embankment to the bottom of the falls. Wood sorrel lined the ravine. The dense woods made it very difficult for strands of sunshine to filter through the trees.

Gibbs Falls. We climbed onto the rocks below the deep, gentle pool at the bottom of the falls. The falls are not that high, perhaps 40 feet. The rocks across the brook are small and pointy. We didn't find a good stone table, so this isn't the best of picnic spots. No one disturbed our solitude during this visit, but I had found this spot well-populated with onlookers and swimmers a year earlier on descending from Mount Clinton. Come to relax, enjoy the falls, and escape.

This hike provides little challenge but is a nice way to take a short hike in the woods and leave the traffic of US 302 behind.

DIANA'S BATHS

General Trail Description

This is a short hike along a gravel road to Diana's Baths on the Lucy Brook.

Trail Statistics

Starting Elevation	500'
Maximum Elevation	600'
Total Vertical	100'
Total Distance	0.4 Mile
Blazes	None
Water	Yes

Our Experience

Difficulty	Easy	
Our Pace	Slow	
Enjoyment	Very Good	

Time and Distance	Hours	Miles
To the Baths	:20	0.2
From the Baths	:20	0.2
Total	:40	0.4

Directions to the Trail

The Lucy Farm, a picturesque white farm house with green shutters, lies 2.1 miles from the Gulf station at the intersection of NH 16 and River Road in North Conway. Take River Road to West Side Road north to the Lucy Farm. If coming from the north, the Lucy Farm lies 4.5 miles from West Side Road's junction with US 302. A gravel road leaves west just north of the farm, and, in 0.1 mile, a barricade prevents further auto travel. Park along the side of this road.

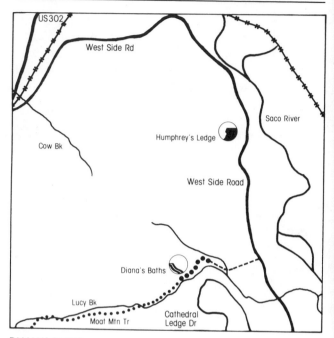

DIANA'S BATHS

DIANA'S BATHS

Diana's Baths, a series of small cascades and shallow pools along the Lucy Brook, are a popular place for people staying in the North Conway area to visit. The shortness of the walk and the varied places on the rocky stone bed to scramble and enjoy the brook make this an excellent short hike for the whole family.

A gravel road off West Side Road can be driven 0.1 mile before access is restricted. We parked along the side of this road and walked the short distance to the baths. The path is a gravel road throughout. Within ten minutes, we approached a wooden structure on our left. Walking past this building and into the woods to our left, we reached the Lucy Brook. A path along the north side of the brook can be followed, or you can scramble out on the rocks and work your way up and down the ledges.

The Baths. The Lucy Brook winds its way along the paths of least resistance, down unique, water-distorted rocky ledges that form the stream's bed. The cirques, hollows, and crevices created by the action of the water on the rock are marvelous. Upstream, a huge, 80-foot-long shelf hinders the water's progress. Water marks on the many crevices had been etched by the stream when high. We were at the baths when the water was low, seeking deep, worn troughs to continue its flow to the Atlantic. In many places the brook flows under rock ledges. Where the water plunges to the stone below, many small bowls have been formed in the granite. On the day we hiked, avoided by the shallow water of the flowing brook, these dishes were filled with rain water.

This is an ideal spot to picnic or to just relax.

Carry out your garbage. Unfortunately, the proximity of Diana's Baths to the road allows access to many who think nothing of littering this scenic area.

Mount Chocorua from Boulder Loop Ledges

SABBADAY FALLS

General Trail Description

The trail for Sabbaday Falls leaves the Sabbaday Falls Picnic Area, travels to the falls, and returns along the same path.

Trail Statistics

Starting Elevation	1400′
Total Vertical	None
Total Distance	0.6 Mile
Blazes	None
Water	Yes

Our Experience

Difficulty	Very Easy
Our Pace	Moderate
Enjoyment	Very Good

Time and Distance	Hours	Miles
NH 112 to the Falls	:20	0.3
Falls to NH 112	:20	0.3
Total	:40	0.6

Directions to the Trail

The trail to Sabbaday Falls leaves the Sabbaday Falls Picnic Area which is located on the south side of the Kancamagus Highway, 3.2 miles west of its junction with Bear Notch Road.

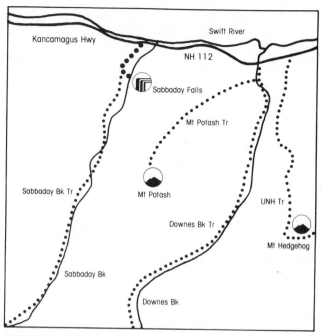

SABBADAY FALLS

SABBADAY FALLS

How the Falls Were Named. Sabbaday Falls, said to have been discovered by early pioneers on a Sunday, thus acquired their name of "Sabbath Day Falls". They are easily reached by a short walk through a pleasant woods. This could be a wonderful introduction to the White Mountains were it not for one drawback—litter.

Our day was magnificent. The temperatures were in the lower 70's, there was no wind at all, and not a cloud could be seen.

The trail to the falls is not a typical mountain footpath. It has been graded, graveled, and widened for easy walking. The trail follows the west bank of the Sabbaday Brook, which is accessible all along the path by short diversions to the left. The water is as clear and clean as any you will find. Go down to the stream and take a drink. Spring water is just one of many pleasures when hiking in the White Mountains.

The Falls. Within ten minutes from the Sabbaday Picnic Area, we approached the falls. You can take a path left or continue straight. Either choice will lead you to a number of lookouts of the falls. Wooden fences have been constructed to prevent accidents to over-anxious young ones (and adults?).

The first of the two upper falls has cut a noticeable chasm in the rock. It is such forces, year after year, that eventually cut deep gouges in the solid granite. The upper falls drop 40 feet to a still pool below. Here the water is diverted 90 degrees to a steep stone gorge. Rushing, it descends through this deeply-cut flume to the lower falls.

Bring your camera to record these picturesque cascades.

Litter. My one reservation in recommending this area is very simple—people who litter. The proximity of the falls to the Kancamagus Highway make them easily accessible to the masses who travel along this road by car, van, and motorcycle. It would seem that an area of such natural beauty would make people aware of their responsibility to respect and protect the environment. Unfortunately, this is not the case. Styrofoam cups float in the pools, cigarette butts collect in the stills of the water, pop cans line the trail, bread wrappers cling to the rocks, and broken glass litters the banks of the brook.

For the most part, people who hike in the White Mountains are very aware of their environment and give it the respect it deserves. The motto in the mountains, "Carry In, Carry Out", is strictly observed. Very seldom will you find litter of any sort along the trails. However, any time an area can be reached with little effort, the garbage collects. Don't let the litter of Sabbaday Falls deter you from further explorations in the White Mountains. You'll find the other trails, those that require more exertion and a strong sense of purpose, free of all trash.

General Trail Description

This is a short hike to a series of ledges overlooking Jackson and the surrounding peaks. Return is by the same path.

Trail Statistics

Starting Elevation	700'
Maximum Elevation	920'
Total Vertical	220'
Total Distance	1.4 Miles
Blazes	Signs with Arrows
	Yellow Ribbons
Water	No

Our Experience

Difficulty	Easy	
Our Pace	Slow	
Enjoyment	Good	
Time and Distance	Hours	Miles
To the Ledge	:30	.7
Return from the Ledge	:25	.7
Total	:55	1.4

Directions to the Trail

From NH 16, turn east through the covered bridge in Jackson and immediately turn right on Dinsmore Road marked, also, by a sign for the Robinwood Inn. Follow this road 0.3 mile to a spot above the inn and park at a grassy area before the Cedar Cottage.

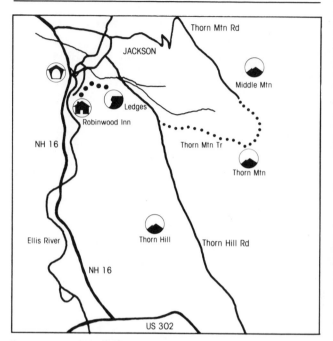

WIGGLESWORTH LEDGE

WIGGLESWORTH LEDGE

The Robinwood Inn. The Robinwood Inn is private property. It is a riding inn, so stay on the footpaths and don't walk on the bridle paths. The ledge, a prominent bluff to the north, is clearly seen from the parking area behind the main building of the inn. The vertical is minimal, making this a good climb for the uninitiated.

The day we climbed there were some clouds, but the visibility was still good. It was cool, in the upper 60's.

From the parking area behind the inn, a road, closed to auto traffic, leads right, past the Pine Cove Cottage, to a horse barn and a carriage barn. Turning left off the road at the horse barn, we saw a simple sign for THE LEDGES marking the trail.

A number of bridle paths diverge from the main path along its course to the ledges. Whenever there might be some confusion, look for small signs with arrows pointing the way to the ledges. If you come across horses, don't step off the path into the woods. Stay on the trail so the horses can see you. They become easily frightened if they're surprised by people off the paths.

The trail begins through an evergreen woods on a delightful, easy-to-follow path. The open areas along the trail allow floods of sunlight to bathe the path.

The first ten minutes of our hike were over level terrain. The trail then crosses a small stream and begins a slight ascent. The vertical soon becomes steeper as the trail winds through a hardwood forest of oak, maple, and beech. A high point is reached after which the trail descends slightly, bears left, and begins the final vertical to the ledges.

Wigglesworth Ledge. The first series of ledges are bordered by iron railings. Here we had a fine view of Mount Washington to the north. Following along the ledges, various views west and south take in Jackson and the surrounding valley. The Moat Mountains lie prominently to the south. Ski slopes scar the side of Mount

Attitash. Directly to the west lies Iron Mountain with Duck's Head forming the bluff directly above the Iron Mountain House. NH 16 winds its way south through Jackson. The pastures and buildings of the Robinwood Inn stand out below.

Travel along the ledge to find a favorite place to stop, rest, and enjoy the view. The descent is very short and easy, so there's no need to hurry.

WINNIWETA FALLS

General Trail Description

The Winniweta Falls Trail lies north of Jackson on NH 16.
The trail leads to Winniweta Falls, a cascade on the Miles
Brook. The trail to the falls and the return are made along
the same path.

Trail Statistics

Starting Elevation	980'
Maximum Elevation	1200'
Total Vertical	220'
Total Distance	2 Miles
Blazes	None
Water	Yes

Our Experience

Difficulty	Easy
Our Pace	Very Slow
Enjoyment	Excellent

Time and Distance	Hours	Miles
NH 16 to the Falls	:45	1
Falls to NH 16	:30	1
Total	1:15	2

Directions to the Trail

The trail leaves along NH 16, 3.1 miles north of the
covered bridge in Jackson and 6.5 miles south of the AMC
Pinkham Notch Camp. A White Mountain National Forest
sign for Winniweta Falls marks the trail on the west side
of NH 16.

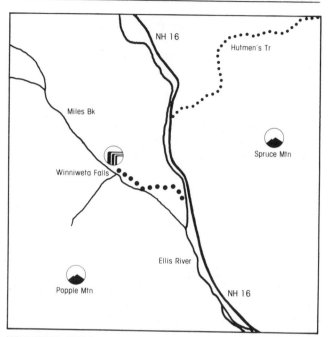

WINNIWETA FALLS

WINNIWETA FALLS

Winniweta Falls are formed by the waters of the Miles Brook. The trail to the falls is excellent and easy hiking even with very small children.

We climbed this trail in early July. The weather was ideal—temperatures in the upper 70's, clear skies, and a slight breeze.

Crossing the Ellis. The trail leaves NH 16 on the west side of the road and comes immediately to the Ellis River. The AMC Guide states "not easy during high water." Truly, I doubt if the river can be crossed at any time without getting wet. We all took off our boots and left them on the rocks on the east side of the Ellis, crossing the river in shallow water by locating flat rocks just below the water's surface.

Barefooted, we entered the woods. The level trail passes through open meadows before beginning a gradual ascent through a young woods. The path through the meadows was lined with wild flowers. White yarrows, flowers that grow in profusion along the highways, lined the path. Hawkweed, an orange flower on a bare stem once believed to be eaten by birds of prey to strengthen their eyesight, grew in the fields. Heal-alls, a purple flower that "if one had heal-all one had no need for a surgeon" bloomed. Small, yellow, vine-like Cinquefoils grew in the meadow. Identifying these wild flowers slowed our progress.

Miles Brook. In a half-hour, after a crawling pace, we came to Miles Brook on our left. The trail begins a very gradual ascent, somewhat away from, and to the right of, the brook. The woods were sparse and young. Fifteen minutes later, we came to a sign to the left of the trail indicating a side path to the falls. The sign had an arrow pointing left and someone had scratched FALLS above the arrow.

Winniweta Falls. The side path, poorly marked, leads quickly to the pools at the bottom of the falls. You can easily scramble out on the rocks to view the water rushing over the stair-like granite to the quiet pools below. The falls, about 40 feet in height, are very pleasant.

The children loved throwing rocks into the lower pool. This seems to be the major attraction of any falls for children. Our son noticed dozens of black and white butterflies on the rocks at the edge of the brook.

We had some fruit on the rocks and soon left, returning at a much more reasonable pace to the Ellis River. Our boots were still there.

This hike is ideal for both children and adults. It is short and has no difficult vertical. The falls are a very definite goal for the kids and crossing the Ellis offers an unusual challenge. The trail travels through open spaces with a variety of wild flowers. Bring a snack to have at the falls; there really isn't much room on the rocks for a family picnic. Our younger child particularly enjoyed this hike, leading the way back for all of us. Winniweta Falls is easy hiking for the smallest member of your family.

Winniweta Falls

BALD MOUNTAIN

General Trail Description

This hike is a circuit from the highway, NH 18, to Bald Mountain, over a ridge to Artist Bluff, and back to the highway at a point about 0.3 mile east of the starting point.

Trail Statistics

Starting Elevation	2000'
Maximum Elevation	2368' (Artist Bluff)
Total Vertical	500'
Total Distance	1.5 Miles
Blazes	None
Water	No

Our Experience

Difficulty	Easy
Our Pace	Slow
Enjoyment	Fair

Time and Distance	Hours	Miles
NH 18 to Bald Mt	:20	.4
Bald Mt to Artist Bluff	:40	.6
Artist Bluff to NH 18	:20	.5
Total	1:20	1.5

Directions to the Trail

NH 18 junctions with US 3, 0.6 mile north of the parking area for Cannon Mountain and 1.3 miles south of the junction of US 3 with I 93. Take NH 18 west 0.4 mile to the sign for the Peabody Ski Slopes. Park opposite the slopes on the north side of the highway.

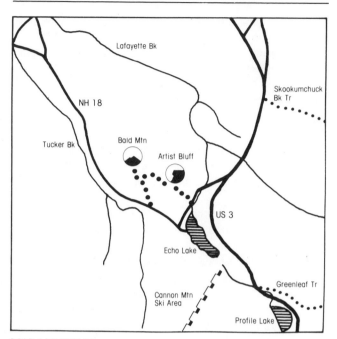

BALD MOUNTAIN

BALD MOUNTAIN

If you're after the shortest mountain climb in the White Mountains, try Bald Mountain. From the highway, NH 18, you can easily see the appropriately named Bald Mountain rising distinctly above the parking area across from the Peabody Ski Slopes. At approximately 2300 feet in elevation, the walk to the peak takes only 20 minutes! A short ridge running east from Bald Mountain leads to Artist Bluff.

The day we started this hike there was a slight breeze, a cloudless sky, and temperatures in the upper 70's. It eventually reached almost 90 degrees, very warm for this area.

We crossed the parking lot and came to a wide, road-like path leading into the woods. There was no sign, but the trail was obvious. The wide path, strewn with small rocks, rises moderately. Small maples line the trail. Within ten minutes we came to a branch in the trail and a sign, **BALD MOUNTAIN 0.2 MILE**, pointing left.

We turned left. Shortly, the path leaves the woods. We scrambled up loose rocks and small boulders toward the summit. The trail takes another sharp left onto unmarked ledges. Climb them any way you can to the open summit.

Bald Mountain. Below you is Echo Lake. To the northeast is the hooked peak of Mount Garfield. The three peaks to the southeast, from north to south, are Lafayette, Lincoln, and Little Haystack. These peaks, along with the not visible summits of Liberty and Flume further south, form the eastern wall of Franconia Notch. Below Little Haystack is a seemingly small, rectangular patch in the trees. This is Shining Rock Cliff, a smooth, unbroken sheet of granite, 200 feet high and 800 feet wide.

Returning to the original trail junction for Bald Mountain, we turned left and proceeded through the woods, traveling the ridge that connects with Artist Bluff. As we walked toward Artist Bluff, more of the view south through Franconia Notch became visible.

The forest was alive with wood sorrel, ferns, and seedlings. Birches sprout from the soil forming on boulder tops. The ridge, a series of ups and downs with frequent outlooks to the right, was easy hiking. Within half an hour, we began a continuous descent. You can easily be diverted from the main trail by many side paths to the cliffs. These side trails were quite overgrown, but we negotiated a few of them to various views through the notch below.

Artist Bluff. Forty minutes after leaving Bald Mountain, we came to the top of a gully filled with boulders and loose rock. Here we found a path left, across the gully, leading us to Artist Bluff. From the bluff there was another good view of the Franconia Range. Further down the notch to the south, the pointed peak of Liberty had become visible.

You'll probably encounter rock climbers on the bluff. This is a popular place for beginners to practice this precarious sport.

Returning to the main trail, we stumbled down the rocks in the gully. Don't be diverted by any side paths. We were, and found ourselves having a difficult time following a not-well-traveled trail through the woods. We came out at the bottom of the slide which, hindsight told us, would have been the preferable way to descend. Five minutes later we emerged on NH 18, very close to its intersection with US 3. A short walk west along the highway led us back to our car.

This is an easy hike. How often can you climb a mountain in 20 minutes? The one complaint we have is the trail to Artist Bluff. It is not marked, and the frequent side paths make the trail very difficult to follow. Obviously, this area is popular for exploring the surrounding cliffs and ledges. These side paths can easily lead you astray and thwart your well-planned, short hike.

THOMPSON FALLS

General Trail Description

This trail is a short climb ending at Thompson Falls. The water from the falls drains, with other streams from Wildcat Mountain, to form the Peabody River. A nature loop can be started on the way to the falls and completed on the return.

Trail Statistics

Starting Elevation	1900'
Maximum Elevation	1975'
Total Vertical	75'
Total Distance	1.2 Miles
Blazes	None
Water	Yes

Our Experience

Difficulty	Easy	
Our Pace	Very Slow	
Enjoyment	Good	
Time and Distance	Hours	Miles
To the Falls	:40	.6
From the Falls	:40	.6
Total	1:20	1.2

Directions to the Trail

The trail leaves from the base of the Wildcat Mountain Ski Area which is located 0.8 mile north of the AMC Pinkham Notch Camp and 2.0 miles south of the Glen House site on NH 16. The ski area, on the east side of the highway, provides plenty of parking. Walk across the bridge over the Peabody and immediately turn left.

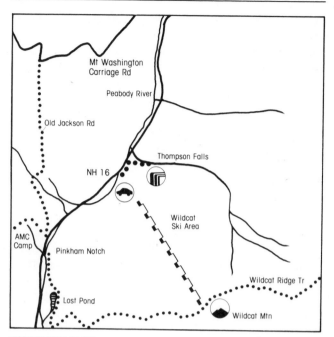

THOMPSON FALLS

THOMPSON FALLS

Wildcat Mountain. The Wildcat Mountain Ski Area is a popular tourist attraction in the summer. The gondola to the top of the mountain can be taken for a fee. Save yourselves some money and climb to the top of Wildcat over the Wildcat Ridge Trail. For a shorter hike with your whole family, take the trail to Thompson Falls. You'll have the added bonus of a guided nature tour along the path that forms the beginning of the trail to the falls.

The day we hiked to Thompson Falls the temperatures were in the lower 70's, and the sky was perfectly blue. The only negative of the day was a number of black flies that didn't realize the Fourth of July had passed.

The Way of the Wildcat. Pick up a pamphlet called "The Way of the Wildcat" from a plastic box at the start of the Thompson Falls Trail. This pamphlet describes 22 stops along the half-mile nature loop, providing information about the forest community, its life and death. You can pause at the first 11 stops on your way to the falls and, taking a path to your left on the way back, stop at the remaining 11.

The first five stops are along the Thompson Falls Trail. The next two stops are on a side path left that leads down to the waters of the Peabody River. Note particularly the mountain ash. We have seldom seen a tree of this variety this tall in the White Mountains. You'll find these trees in the most unlikely places during your travels, mostly growing right out of the cracks of large rocks and ledges.

Thompson Falls. Where the nature loop turns right, we continued straight ahead. The trail descends slightly, crosses a stream on a sturdy, man-made bridge, and soon comes to a road. We crossed the road and entered the woods on the other side. Following the brook on our left, we reached the pool formed by the lower falls in about ten minutes. Continuing up the right bank of the brook, we came to a two-log foot bridge across the water. Crossing the bridge, we climbed the moderately steep left bank of the brook to the upper falls and scrambled out on the rocks. Through the clearing formed by the mountain stream there was a fine view of Mount Washington.

Washington, the highest mountain in the state, is the third highest peak east of the Mississippi. It is the highest mountain east of the Mississippi and north of the Carolinas. The deep ravine to your left is Tuckerman, famous for spring skiing. We saw snow in the ravine in July and suspect some snow remains all through the summer months. The ravine to your right is Huntington. Both ravines host foot trails to the summit of Mount Washington. If you want to spend an arduous yet pleasurable day, plan a hike to the summit of Washington.

The falls are a good place to rest and forget the bustle of the "real world". You are guaranteed privacy. Many times we have taken this trail and have never seen another soul.

The easy return brings you back to the nature trail loop. We turned left and continued our guided tour. As you come to the end of this hike, note the hobblebush at stop 22. You'll see this vine-like shrub along many of the trails in the White Mountains. Often it grows along with seedling, striped maples. Both have broad leaves, but the maples are characteristically lobed. Look for this type of vegetation hugging the paths you travel through the woods.

The Thompson Falls Trail is an excellent introduction to the White Mountains. It can be done by even the youngest member of your family.

CAVE MOUNTAIN

General Trail Description

This trail begins along the Mount Langdon Trail but soon diverges to the left on a separate path. It climbs to the cave at the base of Cave Mountain where it can be followed to the summit ledges. The return is by the same trail.

Trail Statistics

Starting Elevation	700'
Maximum Elevation	1460' (Summit Ledges)
Total Vertical	760'
Total Distance	2 Miles
Blazes	None
Water	No

Our Experience

Difficulty	Moderate to the Cave
	Difficult to the Summit
Our Pace	Slow
Enjoyment	Very Good

Time and Distance	Hours	Miles
Mt Langdon Tr to Cave Mt Tr	:10	.2
Cave Mt Tr to Cave	:25	.5
Cave to Summit	:20	.3
Return from Summit	:30	1.0
Total	1:25	2.0

Directions to Trail

At the intersection of US 302 and Bear Notch Road in Bartlett, go north (as if continuing on Bear Notch Road), past the Bartlett Hotel, 0.4 mile to a T shortly after crossing a bridge over the Saco River. Turn right and park in a cleared area immediately on your right. The Mount Langdon Trail starts across the road from this cleared area.

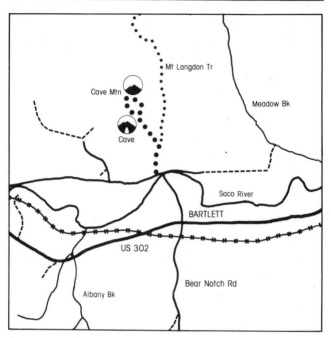

CAVE MOUNTAIN

CAVE MOUNTAIN

The hike to Cave Mountain is one your whole family will enjoy. The children will especially like the adventure and anticipation of reaching the cave at the base of the summit ledges. The summit provides a picturesque view of the town of Bartlett below and is an ideal, private place for a picnic.

The Mount Langdon Trail. A sign for the Mount Langdon Trail clearly marks the starting point for this hike. The trail begins on a wide logging road that rises gradually through the woods. Along the side of the road we encountered a variety of wild flowers. If you're climbing in August, this is also a favorite spot to pick raspberries. You may have to continue along the Mount Langdon Trail above the departure point for Cave Mountain, but you'll be rewarded by finding an abundance of berry bushes.

Within ten minutes after starting along the Mount Langdon Trail, we came to a sign marked, simply, O.5 CAVE, indicating a trail leaving left. Following this path we entered the woods. Ah...a finer forest you will not find. There is a profuse mixture of hardwoods and softwoods—oaks, maples, beeches, birches, hemlocks, pines, and spruce. The variety of lighting through the forest made this an ideal spot for taking pictures.

Within 15 minutes from the CAVE sign, the gradually ascending trail brought us to an area of large boulders strewn on the forest floor. The path travels through these boulders, reaching the largest of them just before the steep ascent to the cave begins. This large boulder, approximately 20 feet long and 15 feet high, marks a favorite spot for the children to explore and for older folks to rest, prolonging the inevitable, difficult scramble to the cave.

Leaves blanket the steep trail to the cave. Gravel, eroded and washed down from the cave entrance, lies under the leaves. You won't find much to gain a foothold on, so just lean forward and keep moving. This five-minute climb will bring you smack in front of the gaping, granite cave entrance.

The Cave. Standing inside the cave, we noticed uneasily that there seemed to be no supporting structure for the two huge, fractured shelves of the roof. It didn't bother the kids, however, who crawled into the damp hole to explore its innards. Don't worry—the cave is small inside and there's nowhere to get lost. Porcupines are said to live in the darkness, but the children, fortunately, did not confirm this.

A large tree obstructs the trail to the left. A non-obstructed path leaves along the right side of the cave. Both lead to the open ledges above, but we strongly recommend the trail to the right. It is steep and slippery but not nearly as difficult as the other trail. Stay behind your children and give them a shove when necessary. It's a tough, 20-minute scramble to the top, but you'll find it worth the effort.

The Ledges Overlooking Bartlett. The open ledges of the summit afford a lovely view of the town of Bartlett nestled in the valley below. The Saco River flows gently through the town toward its junction with the Ellis River to the east in Glen. The highway twisting through the mountains to the south is Bear Notch Road. The bumpy ridge of Bear Mountain forms the eastern side of Bear Notch. The pointed summit of Mount Chocorua was seen far to the south. The Moat range was visible to the southeast.

Plan to picnic here. We have yet to encounter anyone else at this idyllic spot.

The descent to the cave requires care. Once there, the kids will invariably choose to slide down the trail on their bottoms to the boulders below. If you can't tolerate dirty pants, you've come to the wrong trail.

The return to the Mount Langdon Trail from the boulder area is very easy and pleasant. You can be down from the summit ledges in half an hour.

We have climbed the trail to Cave Mountain many times. The children never tire of this hike; they love to explore the cave. The summit ledges provide an ideal spot to relax and enjoy the views.

LOOKOUT LEDGE

General Trail Description

The Ledge Trail ascends to Lookout Ledge on the southern
slope of Mount Randolph. Return is by the same trail.

Trail Statistics

Starting Elevation	1300'
Maximum Elevation	2240'
Total Vertical	940'
Total Distance	2.6 Miles
Blazes	Orange
Water	No

Our Experience

Difficulty	Moderate
Our Pace	Slow
Enjoyment	Very Good

Time and Distance	Hours	Miles
To Notchway Trail	:30	.7
Notchway to Pasture Path	:20	.4
Pasture Path to Ledge	:10	.2
Return from Lookout Ledge	:40	1.3
Total	1:40	2.6

Directions to the Trail

A road turns right, 4.5 miles west along US 2 from where
US 2 and NH 16 separate in Gorham. Follow this road
west 1 mile to the former site of the Ravine House. At the
western edge of the site, the Ledge Trail leaves a short
distance up a gravel driveway. Park off the road on a
gravel area where the driveway meets the road.

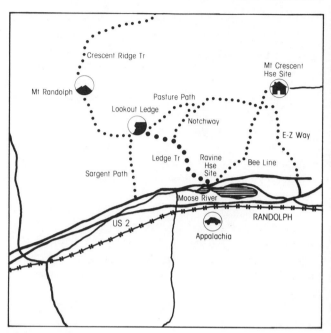

LOOKOUT LEDGE

LOOKOUT LEDGE

Lookout Ledge is an outlook on the south slope of Mount Randolph. From the ledge there is, perhaps, the best view obtainable of King Ravine on Mount Adams. This moderately difficult hike is one the whole family will enjoy.

We climbed on a beautiful day. The temperatures were in the lower 70's, and there was a slight breeze. There were a number of thin, white clouds in the sky.

The trail begins over a stream bed. The footing was difficult over this wet, marshy area. At the top of this damp region, the trail turns left, crosses in front of a private residence, and enters the woods. Here begins a delightful hike through a fine hardwood forest. We encountered some muddy spots, but nothing too serious. Well-marked by orange blazes on the trees, the trail was easy to follow. The ascent was steady but not difficult. We moved slowly and enjoyed the woods of beech, birch, and maples.

After a half-hour, we reached a sign-marked junction with the Notchway Trail. Turning left, we continued the steeper ascent along the Ledge Trail. The older woods give way to an area of newer growth. The path follows a former logging road; a wide swath through the young woods. After 50 minutes, we reached a junction with the Pasture Path.

The Eyrie. Again turning left, we climbed steeply through an evergreen forest. The smell of the needles was marvelous on this summer day. Shortly, we came to an outlook marked The Eyrie. From here there was a fine view of Mount Madison. The trail soon descends to Lookout Ledge at a point marked by a sign on a tree.

Lookout Ledge. Lookout Ledge is a fine place for a picnic. The bugs were a bit pesky, but not enough to drive us away. The views were very good.

The rocky summits of Madison and Adams are the most prominent peaks visible from the ledge. The northern Presidentials were all visible: Pine Mountain (a spur of Mount Madison to the far north), Mounts Madison, Adams, and Jefferson. The Caps on Jefferson were clearly seen along the ridge leading to the summit. There was a superb view of King Ravine below the summit of Mount Adams. Even from this distance, the boulders scattered on the floor of the ravine were clearly visible. Imagine climbing the King Ravine Trail up the headwall of the ravine, 1300 vertical feet in less than 1/4 of a mile! US 2 meanders through the valley below.

Leaving the ledge, we had an easy, delightful hike back. We enjoyed the woods as we walked at a leisurely pace to the trail's start. Driving west along US 2, we could easily recognize the rocky ledge where we had picnicked.

This is a fine hike for families. It is easy and rewarding for everyone.

Bear Notch and Bartlett from Cave Mountain

MOUNT STANTON

General Trail Description

The summit of Mount Stanton is reached along the Mount Stanton Trail. The trail continues on to Mounts Pickering and Langdon, but we retraced our steps from Mount Stanton to the trail's start.

Trail Statistics

Starting Elevation	600'
Maximum Elevation	1748'
Total Vertical	1148'
Total Distance	3.2 Miles
Blazes	None
Water	No

Our Experience

Difficulty	Difficult
Our Pace	Rapid
Enjoyment	Very Good

Time and Distance	Hours	Miles
To Summit	:55	1.6
Return from Summit	:45	1.6
Total	1:40	3.2

Directions to Trail

A road leaves US 302 on the north side, 1.7 miles west of the separation of US 302 and NH 16 in Glen and 0.3 mile east of the Meadowbrook Motel. Follow this road into an area known as Birchview on the Saco, 0.2 mile to a sign for the Mount Stanton Trail on your right. Park along the side of the road.

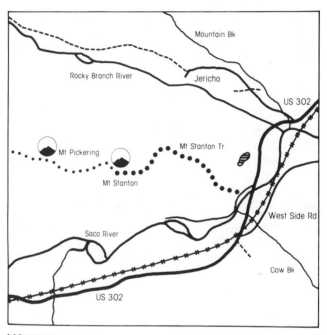

MOUNT STANTON

MOUNT STANTON

Mount Stanton, the southernmost mountain of the Montalban Range, is only 1748 feet in elevation. The short climb to the summit, however, is decidedly difficult. Its rocky, sparsely tree-covered summit affords good views in many directions, making it an ideal climb to initiate families to the rigors of hiking in the White Mountains.

We climbed Mount Stanton on a very hot and humid day. The temperatures were in the upper 80's; no breezes stirred to alleviate our suffering.

The trail leaves the north side of the main road into Birchview by the Saco, travels a short distance through some woods, and comes out on another road in this subdivision. This road ascends moderately giving an excellent view of Mount Stanton. Tell the children that is where they'll be in an hour or so.

A sign to the right points into the woods. After a very short distance, the trail emerges, crosses a gravel road, and enters the woods leaving graded, man-made ways behind.

The trail leads to a low, swampy area—fine for bugs, bad for people. Try to skirt around this area to keep your boots dry. The path becomes a wide, dirt trail through a woods of beech and birch. Yellow blazes throughout made the path easy to follow.

After 15 minutes of a moderate ascent, we turned left and continued to gain altitude. Look for a sharp turn right. This marks the beginning of a difficult, steep climb that took us ten minutes. You'll see the trail rising steeply ahead of you. The composition of the path made this ascent especially difficult. The soil, formed from the decay of rocks, is loose and sandy. It was difficult to gain a good footing, and we relied heavily on the trees along the path for support. During our descent of this section, the kids decided to slide down on their bottoms.

The Ledges. This difficult section ends where the trail veers sharply left. A short walk brought us to the ridge of Stanton overlooking the Saco River to the south. The Saco, originating on Mount Webster ten miles to the north, merges with the Ellis River in Glen and continues its flow to the Atlantic. The river, named by the Pequawket Indians who once inhabited the area, is said to mean ''a snake-like stream running midst pine trees.''

An easy walk along the ridge led us to a number of out-looks to the south and east. The mountain scarred with ski slopes is Attitash. Within ten minutes, following the yellow markings on the rocks, we left the ridge, turning right into the woods. The trail soon becomes steeper. After a very difficult five minute scramble, we were relieved to finally reach the level, rocky summit.

The Summit of Mount Stanton. Traveling past the first open area on our left, we climbed out on the second ledge. This rocky expanse extends tens of feet outward and provides many places to sit and enjoy the views.

The summit was covered with small red oaks. This is unusual in these mountains, but the low altitude and the dry, rocky conditions of Mount Stanton allow these trees to survive where other varieties cannot.

To the east, the tallest peak is Kearsarge North. Across the road is Mount Attitash. Looking west, a number of tall peaks loom. The close, many-humped mountain is Bear Mountain, forming the eastern wall of Bear Notch. To the west of Bear Mountain is the huge mass of Carrigain, a familiar sight along US 302 when traveling north toward Crawford Notch. Further, to the north of Carrigain, are the flatly connected peaks of Mounts Willey (left) and Field (right).

Don't spend all your time here. This is the best outlook south from Stanton, but you should continue along the trail. The summit is broad, and the level path along it gives a number of interesting outlooks. In particular, an outlook north gives views of Doublehead (in Jackson), Washington, Wildcat, and Carter Dome.

On our descent, the sandy trail made for unsure foot-ing. We took our time down the two steep areas and enjoyed the woods. On the way up, since your time is spent huffing and puffing up the steep slopes, it's much more difficult to appreciate the forest.

This is a fine hike. We encountered no one on the trail and wondered why. It has much to offer—a challenging climb, a quick reward in the form of the ridge leading to the peak, and good views from the open summit. It is tough going for little ones but, with patience and a little help from you, they'll make it. This is a guaranteed pleasure-producing hike.

ARETHUSA FALLS

General Trail Description

This hike is along the Arethusa Falls Trail to Arethusa Falls. The return is along the same trail to its junction with the Bemis Brook Trail. This trail is taken down to Bemis Brook and followed back to the junction with the Arethusa Falls Trail very near its starting point.

Trail Statistics

Starting Elevation	1300'
Maximum Elevation	2200' (Top of Falls)
Total Vertical	900'
Total Distance	3 Miles
Blazes	None
Water	Yes

Our Experience

Difficulty	Easy
Our Pace	Slow
Enjoyment	Very Good

Time and Distance	Hours	Miles
To the Falls	1:00	1.4
From the Falls	:45	1.6
Total	1:45	3.0

Directions to the Trail

A gravel road leaves the west side of US 302, 8.3 miles north of the Bartlett Hotel and 3.4 miles south of the Willey House site. There is a sign, **ARETHUSA FALLS**, at the entrance to the road. Take this road 0.1 mile to a parking area just east of the RR tracks.

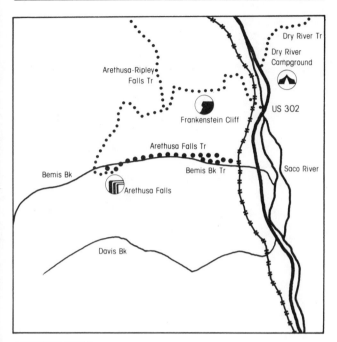

ARETHUSA FALLS

ARETHUSA FALLS

The hike to Arethusa Falls is fine indeed. The 700 feet of vertical to the falls occur over 1.5 miles, making it easy treading for even the youngest child. The circuit back on the Bemis Brook Trail gives a different perspective for the return.

We hiked on a warm day with high humidity and temperatures in the upper 80's. Wading in the Bemis Brook on our return made the day a success despite the heat.

After crossing the RR tracks at the parking area, the trail is marked by a sign, **ARETHUSA FALLS, 1.5 MILES**. Shortly, within hearing distance of the water, a junction with the Bemis Brook Trail leaves left. Continue straight on the Arethusa Falls Trail. The path begins a steady, gradual ascent. It veers away from the Bemis Brook and is soon very high above the water. Climbing through a hardwood forest, we met the return junction with the Bemis Brook Trail in 20 minutes.

The path thins considerably and travels narrowly along the steeply-sloping mountain side. Watch your footing. You can roll a long way down the ravine to the brook! Displacing the hardwoods, spruces line the trail. Now that you have completed the major vertical, it is easy going along this level stretch.

Forty minutes after our start, we crossed a stream feeding Bemis Brook. The path was a web of roots, laid bare by heavy trail usage and water-induced soil erosion. After ten minutes of working through this maze, we came to a crossing of the Bemis. The trail continues along the left bank of the brook within hearing distance of the falls. Minutes later, the falls appear through the trees. Turning right near a trail sign, we had reached our goal.

Arethusa Falls. The brook may be low in the summer, but the sheer 200 foot drop is always worth seeing. This vertical fall is the longest of any cascade in the state of New Hampshire.

We had to work hard for a view of the surrounding mountains. A fairly obscure and very steep trail ascends the south side of the falls (to your left when facing them). It's tough climbing but well worth the effort. We soon came out on the rock shelf above the cascade. You can't see down the falls without being part of them, but there is a fine view east, through the trees, of Frankenstein Cliff and the mountains beyond.

If you're brave, you can walk across the top of the falls (at least when the water is low) and down about ten feet to an outlook. From here there is a fine view of the falls and the rock floor below. Wave at your friends for what might be the last time. We continued down this side of the falls and recommend you do not. The path is overgrown, slippery, and steep. I'm certain you'll find the descent much easier if you go back the way you came.

The Bemis Brook Trail. Returning along the Arethusa Falls Trail, we came to the junction with the Bemis Brook Trail in about 25 minutes. We turned right and began a very steep descent toward the brook. Near the water, the trail turns left, following, but not within sight of, the stream. Shortly, the trail comes very close to the brook near a small, picturesque cascade. The water flows over a smooth, unbroken rock surface as wide as the stream bed. This is an ideal place to remove your boots and walk down the brook to Fawn Pool. The children stripped and swam in the pool.

Leaving the brook, we continued along the trail for about five minutes before coming to the junction with the Arethusa Falls Trail. From here it was a short trek to our original starting point.

This is a highly recommended hike. For the adventurous, the short hike to the top of the falls is a real challenge. A swim in the Bemis Brook can be a fitting climax to your day.

THORN MOUNTAIN

General Trail Description

This hike is an ascent of Thorn Mountain with a descent along the same route.

Trail Statistics

Starting Elevation	1100'
Maximum Elevation	2287'
Total Vertical	1187'
Total Distance	2 Miles
Blazes	Red
Water	No

Our Experience

Difficulty	Moderate
Our Pace	Slow
Enjoyment	Good

Time and Distance	Hours	Miles
To the Summit	1:00	1
From the Summit	:45	1
Total	1:45	2

Directions to the Trail

Travel east through the covered bridge in Jackson 0.3 mile to the junction (right) with Thorn Hill Road. Turn south onto Thorn Hill Road for 1.1 miles to a driveway on the left. There is a sign at the head of the drive, GARRISON, and a mailbox with the same name just past the drive. Park along the side of Thorn Hill Road and walk up the driveway to the trail's start.

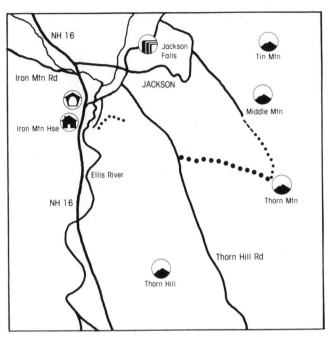

THORN MOUNTAIN

THORN MOUNTAIN

The air was thick and the heat oppressive as we made our way to the trail. Two men were cutting wood near the trail. One said, "No views today, but real good ones on a fine day." The other replied, "Lotta help you are."

Locating the Trail. The trail to Thorn Mountain is indicated by a small sign on the right of a driveway marked **GARRISON**, very near the driveway's junction with Thorn Hill Road. The trail leaves to the right over a grassy path under an apple tree. We immediately crossed a dry brook on a narrow foot bridge. The trail was covered with pine needles. Red blazes mark the well-traveled path. The trail widens at a junction with a former road, but, shortly, the road continues straight while the trail turns sharply left, marked by a crude sign.

The path was clear and unobstructed by rocks. The carpet of needles had changed from pine to spruce. The smell of evergreens was heavy in the air. We approached a crumbling stone wall on our left, remnant of some former boundary marker. The woods, primarily of evergreens, were dotted by an occasional birch. The trail rose steadily. Crudely painted signs with RJA were nailed to the trees, indicating the trail is maintained by the Jackson Resort Association.

As the trail continues to rise, exposed shelves of rock form occasional stretches of the path. More hardwoods begin to appear. Red oaks survive, able to grow at this low altitude among the rocky ledges where other trees cannot.

A Ledge. Forty minutes out, dripping with perspiration, we came onto a broad, open ledge overlooking the village of Jackson. The haze cloaked everything below in a translucent blanket.

From here a steep ascent begins over red-painted, rocky ledges. Red oaks grow in profusion. Within ten minutes from the outlook, the trail winds its way through an area of spruce seedlings and comes to a straight section where a large boulder looms ahead. This landmark was quickly reached. The trail turns left, around the ledge, and over the exposed rock to the open summit.

The Summit of Thorn Mountain. An unpleasant surprise awaited us—a chair lift at the summit. This lift is used to service the ski slopes of Tyrol on the north face of Thorn Mountain. Climbing near the ski slopes, we discovered good views north. Directly to the north are two small mountains. The nearest, with ski chalets scarring its face, is Middle Mountain. Further north from Middle is Tin Mountain. To the northeast, the twin peaks of Doublehead were very prominent. The ski slopes on Black Mountain were visible to the northwest.

Climbing a short distance back along the trail, away from the ski slopes, we came to some fine, open ledges. From here there were good views west. Jackson Village is nestled below. The large mass immediately west is Iron Mountain, its ridge extending east and ending in a bluff known as Duck's Head. Reported to look like a duck's head, we have yet, in the many times we have seen it, to confirm this. The haze was dense enough to prevent us getting a clear look at Iron Mountain even though it was very near. At the base of Duck's Head is the white structure of Iron Mountain House, a small inn in Jackson. To the southwest lies the southern end of the Montalban Ridge. Barely visible was the outline of Mounts Stanton, Pickering, and Langdon (from south to north).

The myth that black flies disappear after the Fourth of July was empirically determined to be just that—a myth. They swarmed around us on this hot day in late August, and we finally conceded and relinquished the territory. Three-quarters of an hour later we were back at Thorn Hill Road.

This hike is short but moderately difficult. You may have to prod your small ones along. The trail is very well-maintained and easy to follow, surely a popular climb in the Jackson area. As the man said when we started, there are "real good" views on a fine day. We couldn't verify his statement.

MOUNT WILLARD

General Trail Description

A short path from the Crawford Depot leads to the Mount Willard Trail. This trail is climbed to Mount Willard with a return by the same route.

Trail Statistics

Starting Elevation	1900'
Maximum Elevation	2804'
Total Vertical	904'
Total Distance	2.8 Miles
Blazes	None
Water	Yes

Our Experience

Difficulty	Moderate
Our Pace	Slow
Enjoyment	Excellent

Time and Distance	Hours	Miles
Depot to the Summit	1:05	1.4
Summit to Depot	:50	1.4
Total	1:55	2.8

Directions to the Trail

Park at the Crawford Depot which is located on the west side of US 302, 2.7 miles north of the Willey House site and 0.1 mile south of the site of the former Crawford House.

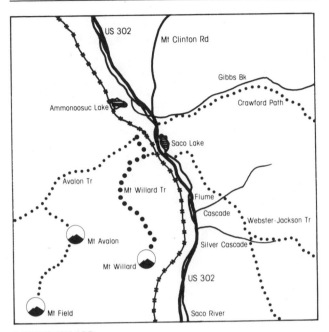

MOUNT WILLARD

MOUNT WILLARD

If your family has time for only one hike in the White Mountains, this is the one to do. The AMC Guide correctly states, "From perhaps no other point in the mountains can so grand a view be obtained with so little effort."

Mount Willard is a northern spur of Mount Field, itself one of the Willey Range. Mount Willey, a huge, awesome mountain, forms the western wall of Crawford Notch. As you travel north through the notch, with Willey on your left and Mount Webster on your right, the sheer rock face of Willard looms straight ahead of you, seemingly an obstruction to your travel. At 2804 feet in elevation, it is not a high mountain, but its unique location gives it a totally unobstructed view south through the notch.

The day we climbed Mount Willard the temperatures were in the 90's with very high humidity. This marked our fifth day in a row of unusually warm weather.

The Crawford House. We parked our car at the Crawford Depot. The Crawford House, abandoned as a hotel in 1976 because of rising fuel costs, formerly stood to the north of the Depot. This hotel was on the site where Thomas Crawford, an early pioneer, first began construction of a large, modern hotel in 1852. The latest structure burned to the ground in the fall of 1977, marking the end of a hundred-year history of grand hotels at this location.

We crossed the RR tracks at the depot and followed a worn path through an open field into the woods and immediately reached a junction. Turning left, we came, in minutes, to another junction with a sign for the Mount Willard Trail.

This trail follows the path of a long-abandoned carriage road to the summit. The wide, stone path is easy hiking. The grades are gradual but steady throughout.

Water. Within five minutes, we approached a stream. Following the left bank of this stream, we came, shortly, to a sign for water. The brook, close to the trail, is easily reached by taking the marked path right.

Continuing along the path, we climbed through a young forest of birch, beech, ash, and aspen. The trail turns left, away from the brook, at a small sign on a tree. We continued steadily over an exposed root path to a point where the trail turns sharply right. Don't go straight here but, rather, follow the rocky bed of the former road. At the top of this rise the trail again turns left and begins a long stretch on a narrow path through a shaded woods. We saw Mount Avalon through the trees to our right.

After 45 minutes, we took a wide left turn through an area that was wet and muddy. After a short distance, the trail turns right. We began a ten minute climb that, leveling off, led directly onto the broad summit of Mount Willard. The children, once having sighted the blue sky through the trees, anxiously ran to the outlook.

The Summit of Mount Willard. The view south through the notch is nothing less than spectacular. The sheer cliffs of Mount Webster rise to the east, and the scarred wall of Mount Willey rises to the west. To the north of the long ridge of Willey lies Mount Field. The low mass of Frankenstein Cliff, at the far end of the notch, finally blocks the view south. Mount Bemis was clearly visible beyond Willey. The small rise to the north of the long ridge of Webster is the summit of Mount Jackson. Appearing lower than Webster, it is actually more than 100 feet higher. With binoculars we could see people crowded on the summit of Jackson. If it's a clear day, walk to the east edge of Willard for a view of the southern Presidentials and Mount Washington to the north.

This is a popular hike. You will probably have plenty of company on the summit. However, the broad ledge will give you ample space to find a quiet spot to relax and enjoy the views.

The descent is very easy. We were down in less than an hour. Willard is a MUST climb. Our younger child first climbed Mount Willard when she was just over three years old. Because of the vertical, some coaxing will be necessary for young children, but this hike is one the whole family will enjoy.

MOUNTAIN POND

General Trail Description

This hike is a loop around Mountain Pond, a picturesque body of water lying east of Jackson.

Trail Statistics

Starting Elevation	1508'
Total Vertical	None
Total Distance	3 Miles
Blazes	None
Water	No

Our Experience

Difficulty	Easy
Our Pace	Moderate
Enjoyment	Fair

Time and Distance	Hours	Miles
To Junction around Pond	:10	.3
Junction to Shelter	:30	.6
Shelter to WMNF Cabin	:35	.8
Cabin to Loop Junction	:45	1.0
Return to Parking	:10	.3
Total	2:10	3.0

Directions to the Trail

Town Hall Road junctions with NH 16, 3.8 miles north of the Gulf station in North Conway. Follow Town Hall Road, which becomes Slippery Brook Road, east from its junction with NH 16, 5.8 miles to the junction with a road left. Continue straight 0.7 mile to a sign on the right for Mountain Pond. Turn right and park in a cleared area off the road. (Note: only the first two miles of Slippery Brook Road are paved.)

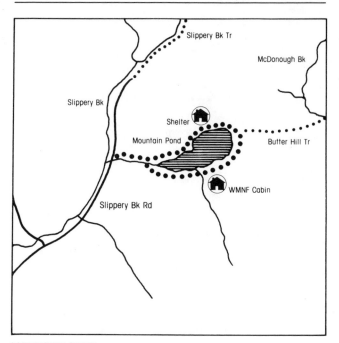

MOUNTAIN POND

MOUNTAIN POND

The trail to Mountain Pond begins near the parking area, follows a wide, former road through a mixed forest and, shortly, comes to a sign marking the junction of the two trails that form a north-south loop around the pond. At this junction, a short side trail leads straight to the pond, a still body of water lying at 1500 feet in elevation.

We chose the left (north) branch. The trail becomes a rough, rocky path where we had to carefully watch our footing. It was not difficult, however, as there was no vertical. The path, although close to the water, does not follow the bank of the pond. There were occasional views of the pond, and many short paths leading to the water's edge.

Bees. We had the misfortune to choose a side path to the water that disturbed a number of ill-tempered bees. They hit .571, stinging four of the seven of us. I think the bees were yellow jackets, but as Winnie-the-Pooh said, "You never can tell with bees." Although the stings were not too painful, they caused considerable swelling. This incident left us in poor spirits, and we continued moving with our small children as rapidly as we could.

A half-hour from the loop junction (0.6 mile), we came to a side path left to the shelter. We took the main path, veered right, and came out on a bank along the water. The trail, turning left, travels along the bank of the pond. This was an excellent breeding ground for mosquitoes, and they swarmed by the hundreds near the shore of the pond. We found bunchberries and wild blueberries growing along the trail. We had many views of Mount Doublehead to the west.

Just under an hour (1.2 miles), we came to a sign marking a trail east to Butterhill Road. The trail around the pond turns right, follows along the eastern shore of Mountain Pond, and passes through a fine hemlock forest.

Returning along the south shore, we came to a fine outlook across the pond to the bare, prominent face of South Baldface. This appeared to be an excellent mountain to climb, and we vowed to do it before the summer was over. We never did.

A Cabin. Twenty minutes from the Butterhill trail junction, we came to a White Mountain National Forest cabin. The kids discovered a well and pump used to supply water to the cabin. The pump and shelter were well-received by the children. They pumped water from the well and used the inside of the cabin as a junglegym. Plan to stay awhile; our children really enjoyed running and playing in and about the cabin.

There were no diversions along the trail from the cabin. Near the loop junction, the trail traverses through a tall stand of spruce. It then crosses a wet, swampy area, over boulders, and eventually meets again with the northern branch of the Pond Loop Trail. From here it was an easy walk to the parking area.

Mountain Pond is quite nice. The views of Mount Doublehead and South Baldface were very good, and the trail along the pond offers unique vantage points to see these peaks. There is no vertical, making the hike easy but, also, a bit tedious. The bees were a decided negative, but maybe you won't encounter them. If you're interested in a moderately long but easy hike, try Mountain Pond.

MOUNT DOUBLEHEAD

General Trail Description

This hike is a loop up the New Path to the south peak of Doublehead, north along the ridge connecting the south and north peaks to the junction with the Old Path, down the Old Path, and out to Dundee Road on the Doublehead Ski Trail.

Trail Statistics

Starting Elevation	1500'
Maximum Elevation	2938'
Total Vertical	1438'
Total Distance	2.7 Miles
Blazes	Cairns on the New Path
Water	No

Our Experience

Difficulty	Moderate to Difficult
Our Pace	Slow
Enjoyment	Very Good

Time and Distance	Hours	Miles
Dundee Road to South Peak	1:20	1.2
South Peak to Old Path	:15	.3
Old Path to Dundee Road	:50	1.2
Total	2:25	2.7

Directions to Trail

From Jackson, take the fork, 16B, toward Black Mountain (northwest) to its intersection with Dundee Road. 2.9 miles from the fork, the New Path leaves Dundee Road. From Intervale, the New Path leaves Dundee Road 4.5 miles from the junction of 16A with Dundee Road. There is a sign, **NEW PATH, SOUTH DOUBLEHEAD** 1.3. It is hard to see, especially if approaching from the south. The trail leaves on the east side of the road directly opposite a small, cedar-shingled shed.

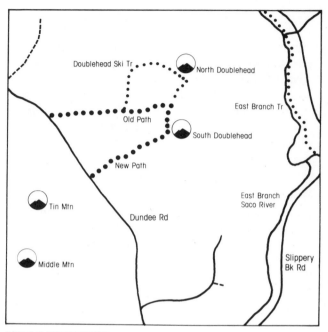

MOUNT DOUBLEHEAD

MOUNT DOUBLEHEAD

Mount Doublehead is a familiar landmark to those from the Jackson area. Easily recognized by its twin summits, it stands prominently against the skyline from many points along Route 16B. Trails climb both summits, but we chose to hike to the south peak. Although not a great distance, the climb is moderately difficult. Once the vertical begins in earnest, there is no let-up until the summit is reached. The views from the summit are very good.

We climbed on a cool, partly sunny day. Clouds obscured our view of Mount Washington from the summit of Doublehead, but the lower peaks were clearly visible.

The New Path. The New Path begins on the east side of Dundee road opposite a small, cedar-shingled shed. It follows a wide logging road and leads left into the woods where the road continues straight. Becoming narrower, the level trail is unobstructed. Cairns mark the way throughout the New Path.

After ten minutes, we crossed the bed of a former brook; no water was available. The trail rises gently through a woods of spruce and fir. Dead trees and limbs, victims of severe, stormy winds, littered the woods. We passed a couple of lone red oaks in a woods of mostly evergreens. We noticed a huge, four-trunked oak—a most unusual sight.

Our Goal. In 25 minutes, we came to the first of two open ledges. Looking straight ahead we clearly saw our destination, the south peak of Doublehead. Following cairns along the ledge, we entered the woods again and quickly came to the second ledge. There were fine views of the mountains to the southwest. The ski slopes of Tyrol on Thorn Mountain in Jackson were very close.

The steep climb begins. The path composition becomes a mixture of sandy, gravelly soil with small boulders imbedded in the dirt. The trail offers many views through the trees. We found the going steep, wet, and VERY slippery. Even with our help, our younger child suffered her share of spills.

The South Peak. Shortly after an hour, the trail veers right and begins a series of short zig-zags ending at the Ridge Trail near the south summit. We turned right and climbed onto an open area marked by a large cairn. To the right of the path you can scramble to a fine outlook with views south and west.

We continued straight along the ridge path to another large cairn and a fine outlook east, with varied views north and south. The nearest peak is the north peak of Doublehead. From Doublehead, heading northeast, are Chandler Mountain and Sable Mountain. The distinctive notch to the north is Carter Notch, separating the long ridge of Wildcat Mountain to the left and the broad, rounded peak of Carter Dome to the right. The pond to the east is Mountain Pond. Lying at approximately 1500 feet in elevation, this small pond is 3/4 mile long and 1/4 mile wide. To the south lie Bartlett Mountain and, a tower visible on its summit, Kearsarge North.

Returning to the first cairn, we ate lunch on the ledges with views west. White Horse and Cathedral Ledges in North Conway appeared insignificant below the Moat Mountains. The pointed peak of Chocorua poked up from behind the Moat Range. The nearer ski slopes are from Tyrol, while the ones in the distance are on Mount Attitash in Bartlett. There is a fine panorama of the Montalban Range extending in an unbroken line from Mount Stanton, south, to Stairs Mountain, north. Passaconaway and Tripyramid were visible far to the southwest. The small peaks, very close, are Tin (closest), Middle, and Thorn.

We left, followed the Ridge Trail past its junction with the New Path, and came to another superb outlook with views west and north toward Carter Notch. The wind came up and caused us to move on quickly. Fifteen minutes from the south peak, we came to a junction with the Old Path. Turning left, we began the descent.

The Old Path. The Old Path was not nearly as wet and slippery as the New Path. Fewer obstacles hindered our progress as we traveled through a still spruce forest. Unlike the New Path, there were no views through the trees.

After half an hour on the Old Path, we came to a junction with the Doublehead Ski Trail. If ascending this way, the ski trail goes left to the north summit, while the Old Path goes right to the junction with the Ridge Trail. We followed the ski trail down through a broadleafed woods. Oaks flourish at these lower altitudes. We saw our first sign of fall in mid August—a fallen, bright red maple leaf.

Fifty minutes after beginning our descent from the col between the south and north peaks, we emerged on Dundee road near a sign for the Doublehead Ski Trail. We walked the short 0.4 mile south along the road to our car.

This is not a hike for a casual family outing. The New Path is quite steep and relentless. However, the woods are very pleasant, the outlooks along the way are fine, and the views from the summit are, perhaps, the best in the Jackson area. Pack a lunch and plan to stay awhile on the top. You'll enjoy a very pleasant day.

Mount Doublehead

PINE MOUNTAIN

General Trail Description

This trail follows a dirt road halfway up the mountain to a junction with **LEDGE TRAIL**. Ledge Trail is followed over the south peak, down to the col between the south and north peaks, to the north peak. We retraced our steps for the descent.

Trail Statistics

Starting Elevation	1650'
Maximum Elevation	2404'
Total Vertical	754'
Total Distance	3.2 Miles
Blazes	None
Water	No

Our Experience

Difficulty	Moderate	
Our Pace	Moderate	
Enjoyment	Fair	
Time and Distance	**Hours**	**Miles**
To South Peak	1:05	1.2
To North Peak	:20	.4
To South Peak and Return	1:10	1.6
Total	2:35	3.2

Directions to the Trail

Dolly Copp Road leaves NH 16, 6 miles north of the AMC Pinkham Notch Camp and 4.5 miles south of the separation of NH 16 and US 2 in Gorham. Take Dolly Copp Road west. After the hardtop surface ends, bear to the left at a fork in the road. 1.9 miles in on Dolly Copp Road the road to Pine Mountain leaves right. Follow this road to a gate restricting access to the mountain and park your car at a small area to the left of the gate.

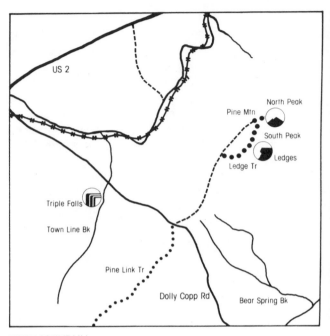

PINE MOUNTAIN

PINE MOUNTAIN

Pine Mountain is the northernmost peak of the Presidential Range. Its height, at 2404 feet in elevation, appears inconsequential compared to the four other northern peaks. Mounts Clay, Jefferson, Adams, and Madison are all over 5000 feet! Although the mountain is privately owned and houses the Douglas Horton Center, a religious retreat associated with the First Church of Christ, the public is welcome to enjoy the views and use the trails, provided there is no overnight camping. There are good views, especially to the east, from the ledges approaching the south summit. The north peak is wooded, but there is an open ledge at the site of an outdoor chapel, Chapel Rock, on the northeast side of the mountain.

Our good weather had ended. Following a dreary day of rain, we hiked on a cloudy, overcast day. The wind made the upper 60's temperature seem much cooler, especially on the ledges. Because of the weather, our hike was not as enjoyable as it might have been.

The first half of this hike is along a dirt road (for authorized vehicles only) that leads to the Douglas Horton Center located on the north summit. An auto road is not like a footpath through the woods; it mars the landscape and gives an urban feeling to the hike.

Paper birches appeared along the road. Striped maples, often seen as vine-like foliage along White Mountain trails, had gained stature in these woods. The bugs had also done well.

The Ledge Trail.   Within half an hour, we came to a sign to our right marked LEDGE TRAIL. We entered the woods and ascended quickly. The forest path gave way to exposed boulders, obstacles to our ascent. Climbing these rocks reminded us of trails to the higher peaks in the White Mountains, since you usually don't meet such terrain until you're at much higher altitudes. The children especially enjoyed this part of the trail. They always love rock climbing, going out of their way to make the ascent as difficult as possible.

The South Ledges.   We soon reached the south ledges. On a good day the views must be fine. On our day the clouds had enveloped Madison, the very nearest northern peak. To the east, Wildcat Ridge was barely visible through the mist.

The trail along the ledges is marked by yellow-painted arrows on the rocks. We saw many mountain ash, some 20 feet high, sprouting from rock crevices along the path.

The trail continues, rather steeply. There are frequent outlooks from the ledges. Once you come to an immense rock ledge, you're near the south summit. Enjoy your last views from the south peak.

The path levels off and crosses the site of a former tower where all that remain are the four cement piers. The trail continues along a spruce-lined path, down to the col between the south and north peaks, and soon joins the auto road near the parking area for the Center. Take the path to your right and, within 200 feet, the trail for Chapel Rock leaves to the right.

Chapel Rock. A stone pulpit has been set on the mountain face of this outdoor chapel. A wooden cross stands alone. To your left are the Carters—North, Middle, and South. Further south lies the rounded peak of Carter Dome, followed by Wildcat Ridge with its five not-so-distinct summits. The low point between Carter Dome and Wildcat is Carter Notch. The one hour climb from this notch to the peak of Wildcat is reputed to be very difficult. From looking at the angle of ascent, this is easy to imagine.

We left and retraced our steps to the broad rock outlook near the south peak. We ate lunch huddled in a crevice between the ledges. A stair-like notch in the granite has etched into the vertical surface CAROL WILLIAMS HORTON. Is it a mountain memorial? Perhaps a tomb?

The return to Dolly Copp Road took us 50 minutes. We maintained a good pace this day; the mist and cold kept us moving.

The lack of a trail from the foot of Pine Mountain is a disadvantage. Once the Ledge Trail is reached, however, the going is fine. The views east and south were marginal for us but must be good on a clear day. Madison seemed to block the view of the other northern peaks, but we'll have to wait for a sunny day on Pine Mountain to be certain.

WHITE HORSE LEDGE

General Trail Description

The highest point and destination of this hike is White Horse Ledge. The hike begins on the Bryce Path to its junction with the White Horse Trail. White Horse Trail is taken to White Horse Ledge, down, and around the south edge of Echo Lake on Around the Lake Trail. This path is taken around the west shore of Echo Lake to the Bryce Link and its junction with the Bryce Path, completing the loop.

Trail Statistics

Starting Elevation	600'
Maximum Elevation	1455'
Total Vertical	855'
Total Distance	3.3 Miles
Blazes	Yellow
Water	No

Our Experience

Difficulty	Bryce Path is Difficult
	Remainder is Moderate
Our Pace	Slow
Enjoyment	Very Good

Time and Distance	Hours	Miles
Bryce Path to White Horse Tr	:40	.6
White Horse Tr to Ledge	:30	.5
Ledge to Bryce Link	1:00	1.4
Bryce Link to Bryce Path	:20	.5
Bryce Path to Parking	:10	.3
Total	2:40	3.3

Directions to the Trail

Turn west on River Road just north of downtown North Conway at a Gulf station. Take this road to a sign for Cathedral Ledge on Cathedral Ledge Drive, 1.4 miles from the junction with River Road. Follow this road toward Cathedral Ledge 0.2 mile to a dirt road left. Follow the dirt road to a parking area. Walk along the road to a sign marking the start of the Bryce Path.

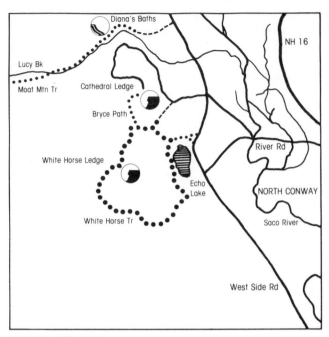

WHITE HORSE LEDGE

WHITE HORSE LEDGE

The Ledges of North Conway. Two low ledges to the west of North Conway are landmarks in the area. They are easily seen when traveling along NH 16 north of the town. The higher ledge, White Horse, is to the south while the lower ledge, Cathedral, is to the north. White Horse is best viewed across Echo Lake from Echo Lake State Park. An auto road leads to the summit of Cathedral Ledge. Both of these sheer rock cliffs are popular for rock climbing.

We climbed White Horse Ledge at the end of June. The temperatures were in the 70's, but the day was rainy. It rained steadily until we reached the ledge where it conveniently stopped, only to begin again on our descent.

Bryce Path. The trail begins from the parking area and climbs easily on a broad path to a three-way junction. To the left is the Bryce Link from around Echo Lake. Straight ahead is the path for rock climbers. We saw three people climbing Cathedral Ledge and realized we weren't the only crazy ones out on this day. We turned right, following Bryce Path. The trail begins a steady, difficult ascent along a rocky, sandy-soiled trail. The boulders were as big as our younger child. They were wet and difficult for her to negotiate. She required much coaxing and lifting.

The woods along the entire trail are notable for an abundance of huge beech trees. Beech, prominent throughout the area, are easily recognized by their pointed, serrated leaves and smooth, gray bark. They will be frequent companions of yours when hiking in the White Mountains.

White Horse Trail. After 0.6 mile, White Horse Trail leaves left. Fifteen minutes from this junction, we came to our first view, through the trees, of Echo Lake. The trail begins an easy stretch through the woods over an open expanse of rock as broad as a wide road. It was finally easy going for everyone.

White Horse Ledge. Eventually the trail enters the woods again and climbs easily to the top of White Horse Ledge. The huge rock summit is covered with scrubby, red pines that obscure the eastern view of the lake and the mountains. Stay left of these trees and picnic on the steep-sloping ledge overlooking Echo Lake below and

North Conway to the east. The Conway area, now the largest community except Berlin in northern New Hampshire, was, in 1672, populated by the Pequawket tribe and their 200 wigwams. Cathedral Ledge is prominent to the north. To the east, the ski slopes of Mount Cranmore can be seen.

We were above the low-lying clouds on the ledges. The mist rolled in as we lunched, leaving us no views.

Following the yellow blazes on the rocks, up the ledge, we began our descent. A sign, barely legible, pointed the way down. The descent was very easy, as there were no boulders obstructing the trail. We walked on a floor of acorns. The rain began in earnest and became a steady downpour, leaving the shrubs and leaves a bright, glistening green. The mosquitoes came out in full force.

The sparse forest was quiet and pleasant. We again encountered huge beeches at the lower altitudes. The kids saw and captured some tree toads that crossed their paths. The toads were relieved, I'm sure, to be sent on their way again.

Forty-five minutes from the ledges, we came to a sea of huge boulders, some 20 to 30 feet in height. Remnants of some long-ago slide, they lined the left of the trail. Can you imagine the thunder created by their fall?

Around the Lake. At the boundary of Echo Lake State Park, we followed the yellow blazes to **AROUND THE LAKE** path. Halfway around the lake we took a few steps to the water's edge and let the children try to catch some of the hundreds of tadpoles swimming there.

The trail turns left on the Bryce Link, away from the lake, and soon joins the Bryce Path.

This hike would have been very enjoyable on a nice day. The children viewed the rain with mixed emotions — fun for awhile but unpleasant after they were thoroughly soaked and cold. The Bryce Path boulders were slippery and difficult for small legs to negotiate. White Horse Ledge, however, is a good, private, open place to lunch or just relax.

BOULDER LOOP

General Trail Description

The Boulder Loop Trail is a three mile loop with 16 marked stops. A leaflet published by the US Forest Service gives descriptive information for each stop along the way.

Trail Statistics

Starting Elevation	900'
Maximum Elevation	1900'
Total Vertical	1000'
Total Distance	2.9 Miles
Blazes	Yellow
Water	No

Our Experience

Difficulty	Easy
Our Pace	Very Slow
Enjoyment	Excellent

Time and Distance	Hours	Miles
To the Ledges	1:45	1.5
Completing the Loop	1:00	1.4
Total	2:45	2.9

Directions to the Trail

The trail starts near the Covered Bridge Campground which is located just off the Kancamagus Highway, NH 112, 5.9 miles east of its junction with Bear Notch Road and 6.4 miles west of its junction with NH 16. Turn north onto Dugway road through the covered bridge crossing the Swift River. Turn right and in 0.1 mile park along the road near the White Mountain National Forest sign for Boulder Loop Trail.

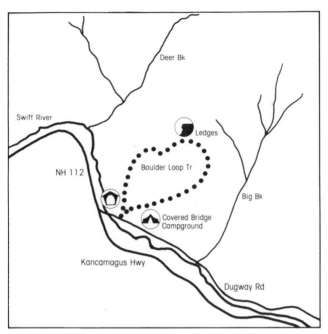

BOULDER LOOP

BOULDER LOOP

A Guided Tour. A pamphlet, published by the US Forest Service, is found in a wooden box at the start of Boulder Loop Trail. It contains a general description of the trail, a map, information on the 16 stops along the trail (marked by yellow-topped posts with white numbers), and a labeled panorama of the Swift River Valley as seen from the ledges on the trail.

The weather was ideal when we climbed Boulder Loop Trail. The temperatures were in the upper 70's, and it was sunny throughout the day.

The Boulders. As you walk by the huge rocks at the start and finish of your hike, you will see that Boulder Loop is an appropriate name. Can you imagine the forces which were unleashed by such boulder slides?

The ascent to the ledges was steady but easy. The woods were magnificent. The wide, well-maintained trail was a pleasure to walk. We stopped frequently to enjoy the woods and the day. Our younger child learned to recognize birches and beeches by their distinctive barks. She took great pride in her accomplishment.

The lower woods are comprised primarily of broadleafed trees. As you climb, evergreens appear in greater numbers, mixed with the hardwoods. The descriptive information in the pamphlet explains the environmental conditions that allow broadleafed trees to proliferate where it is warm and dry, while the conifers prefer the cool, moist soil of the upper regions. The description of soil formation through rock erosion was fascinating and, were it not for glimpses of the on-going process, hard to imagine. One wonders about the destruction and death of huge trees and ponders the many causes: disease, insects, wind, and storms.

We soon reached the first outlook where there were views of the neighboring mountains and the meandering Swift River. We're always amazed at how quickly the heights are reached by merely taking small steps along the trail.

The Ledges. We reached the cliffs after almost two hours. Bring a lunch and plan to stay awhile. The labeled panorama in the Boulder Loop pamphlet makes the views even more enjoyable. Passaconaway looms huge to the southwest. We could easily distinguish the three peaks of Tripyramid to the west. We recognized Mount Osceola lying far to the west. Following the yellow markings on the rocks, we walked the ledges to their eastern-most point where there was a superb view of the rocky cone of Mount Chocorua to the south.

There are many varieties of trees on the ledges. White spruce abound. Mountain ash grow from the rock crevices. A small oak stands alone, against the sky, near the west end of the ledges.

We continued the loop trail by an easy descent. Between stops 12 and 13 the map indicates ash trees. We missed them, so look carefully. The huge hemlock at stop 13 stands alone and stark among the other trees. When you reach the boulder area, it's not far to the trail's end.

This hike is a must. Our children's official chipmunk count was 25. Everyone will enjoy this walk, and the published pamphlet gives an educational bonus.

Oak Tree on Boulder Loop Ledges

MOUNT PEMIGEWASSET

General Trail Description

This hike is a nearly closed loop that ascends Mount Pemigewasset from the south, descends to the north, and returns to US 3 about one mile north of its original starting point.

Trail Statistics

Starting Elevation	1350'
Maximum Elevation	2554'
Total Vertical	1204'
Total Distance	2.3 Miles
Blazes	Indian Head Trail, Red; Pemigewasset Mt Trail, Blue at Summit, Yellow on Trail
Water	No

Our Experience

Difficulty	Easy to Moderate
Our Pace	Slow
Enjoyment	Good

Time and Distance	Hours	Miles
Indian Head Tr to Summit	1:45	1.0
Pemigewasset Mt Tr to US 3	1:00	1.3
Total	2:45	2.3

Directions to the Trail

The Indian Head Trail begins on the property of the Indian Head Cabins, 1.6 miles north of Interstate 93's temporary cessation through Franconia Notch. There is no sign for the cabins, but they appear on the west opposite a small observation tower. A Texaco station is just to the north of the cabins. There is a parking lot on the west side of the road with a small sign stating INDIAN HEAD PARKING. We parked there.

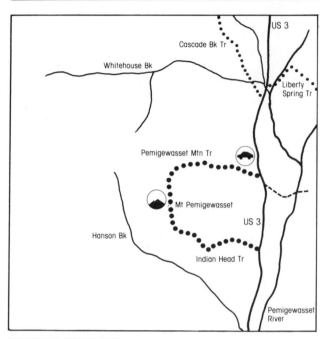

MOUNT PEMIGEWASSET

MOUNT PEMIGEWASSET

Indian Profile. A natural stone profile of an Indian is formed by the ledges on the south shoulder of Mount Pemigewasset. Stop to view the profile before starting your hike. Tell the youngsters they will eventually climb the cliffs that form the profile.

Our day began beautifully with scattered clouds, temperatures in the lower 70's, and cool breezes. We dallied along the Kancamagus Highway taking pictures of wild flowers growing in profusion along the side of the road. By the time we started our climb, it had become cloudy. At the summit, large, black clouds rolled in over Franconia Ridge, confirming, once again, if you don't like the weather in the White Mountains, wait five minutes and it will change.

Once you've parked, you'll see a road around the cabins. Follow it to the south end of the cabins and look carefully for a sign on a tree to your left marking the start of the trail. The trail is unnamed in the AMC Guide, but the sign we found read TRAIL TO INDIAN HEAD.

The Abenaki. The trail sign capsules a bit of history. The Abenaki (misspelled Abernacky) Indians used the ledges forming the top of Indian Head as a lookout post. Pemigewasset was a great chief of the Abenakis, immortalized by Mount Pemigewasset, the Pemigewasset River and, as legend has it, by his profile, Great Stone Face, carved by the Great Spirit into the granite of Cannon Mountain.

The woods were abundant with birches and beeches. Look for striped maples, characterized by green bark with long, white vertical stripes. You'll see many of them starting their growth as vine-like foliage along the trail.

The trail, marked by red blazes painted on the trees, climbs moderately. Within 15 minutes, we approached a stream on our left. For the next half-hour we zig-zagged next to, then away from, the water. At one point the stream flows over a large expanse of flat, moss-covered rocks. The lighting on the rocks made this a good place for taking pictures.

After an hour, we walked over a narrow path overgrown with vines and small trees. This trail is infrequently traveled and poorly maintained. The trail turns right, becomes wider, winds through a much-decayed woods, and leaves all signs of water behind. Large, fallen trees obstructed our way and made the going difficult. The trail becomes rocky and, near the top, large boulders obstruct the path. Our children, as is characteristic of small ones, consistently took the path of most resistance.

Once you catch a glimpse through the trees of the ledges to your right, you don't have much further to go. The trail begins its only steep section, climbing behind the ledges and approaching them from the west. The trail joins the blue-blazed Pemigewasset Mountain Trail and funnels to the open ledges of Mount Pemigewasset.

The Summit of Pemigewasset. The summit offers spectacular views from north to south. We wondered why this peak was unpopulated. Could it be the poorly maintained Indian Head Trail or the inadequately marked Pemigewasset Mountain Trail? It is easy to imagine the use of this mountain as an Indian lookout. Plan to spend time on the summit.

To the south wind the two separated strips of I-93 concrete. To the southeast rise the distinctive peaks of Osceola. We could just make out the tower on the west peak. Walking along the ledges, we came to a northern outlook. To the northeast is Franconia Ridge: Lafayette, furthest north, the distinctively pointed peak of Mount Lincoln, Little Haystack, Mount Liberty, and the southernmost peak, Flume. Rocks, strewn down the face of Flume, are evidence of the flume slide. Up the notch, across from Lafayette, looms the huge outline of Cannon.

The Pemigewasset Mountain Trail. The wind picked up and the clouds became ominous. We quickly gathered our things and headed down. After leaving the ledges, we followed blue blazes to a point where the two trails diverged. Taking the Pemigewasset Mountain Trail, the blue blazes end, and, with the exception of a few yellow blazes midway down, there were no more trail markings. In contrast to the Indian Head Trail, the Pemigewasset Mountain Trail was wide, easy to follow, and well-maintained. It was an easy and pleasant descent through an open woods.

The trail ends at a picnic area west of the parking for the Flume. The sign for the trail is simply marked TRAIL, giving no indication of its length or destination. We had a one-mile walk south on US 3 to our car.

Perhaps the best way to hike this peak is up and down the Pemigewasset Mountain Trail. The Indian Head trail is so poorly maintained, it is hard to recommend.

The summit of Pemigewasset is a well-defined goal for children. Giving fine views, the moderate effort required to climb this mountain makes it a must climb. Franconia Notch is so popular, I'm mystified by the apparent obscurity of this summit to hikers. It's a plus for you; while everyone else is off bagging the big ones, your family can be enjoying the day on top of Pemigewasset.

Daisies along the Kancamagus

General Trail Description

This trail makes a difficult, direct ascent of Owl's Head. It leaves from the rear of the unoccupied, but privately owned, Slide Farm. Descent is by the same route.

Trail Statistics

Starting Elevation	1400'
Maximum Elevation	3370'
Total Vertical	1970'
Total Distance	2.8 Miles
Blazes (sporadic)	Red Ribbons on Trees
Water	No

Our Experience

Difficulty	Very Difficult
Our Pace	Moderate
Enjoyment	Excellent

Time and Distance	Hours	Miles
Slide Farm to Owl's Head	1:40	1.4
Return from Owl's Head	1:15	1.4
Total	2:55	2.8

Directions to the Trail

The driveway leading to the Slide Farm is on the south side of NH 115. From the west, it is 5.7 miles from the junction of US 3 and NH 115. From the east, it is 1.0 mile from the junction of Cherry Mountain Road and NH 115. Cherry Mountain Road is unpaved. If you take it, be prepared for a bumpy ride.

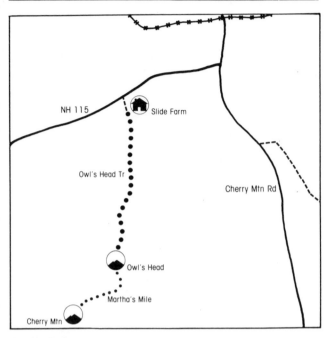

OWL'S HEAD

OWL'S HEAD

This Owl's Head is not to be confused with the more well-known Owl's Head of the Franconia Range. The Owl's Head we climbed, at approximately 3400 feet in elevation, lies northwest of Mount Washington. Its open ledges just beyond the summit offer the finest views of the Presidential Range that we have yet discovered.

A storm the day before put an end to the hot weather. The temperatures were in the 60's. The sky, partly cloudy in the morning, became quite cloudy during the day. Dark, billowing clouds obscured the northern Presidentials by the time we reached Owl's Head.

Locating the Trail. We had a difficult time locating the trail. A fine gentleman by the name of Mr. Hartley lives at the white farmhouse on the southwest corner of the intersection of Cherry Mountain Road and NH 115. He had recently climbed Owl's Head (he was in his eighties!) and gladly gave us directions to, as well as a detailed description of, the trail.

There are two houses to your left as you travel west along NH 115 from its intersection with Cherry Mountain Road. The first is the Hartley farm. Shortly beyond the second house, a gravel driveway leaves left from the highway to Slide Farm. The trail for Owl's Head leaves from the back of the farm. Park along NH 115 and walk in on the driveway 0.2 mile. This is private property, and there is some issue pending as to access to the trail. We found the small farmhouse unoccupied, but the barn had an uninviting **NO TRESPASSING** sign on it. A slight path can be found in the meadow between the house and the barn. Head for the apple tree and stay to the right of it.

The path through the field gradually widens and becomes a noticeable trail. The woods close in around the path. Fifteen minutes from the farm, we turned right at a branch in the trail. Look for a sign, **PATH**, on a tree to your right.

The easy-to-follow trail travels through a beautiful hardwood forest. It begins an unrelenting, steep ascent through the woods. Don't look for any relief; there isn't any. Indian Pipes, white, stem-like flowers, poked up at us from the path. The woods were crowded with huge birches and maples.

The Steep Ascent. After 50 minutes, the trail levels somewhat but, shortly, takes a sharp turn right and begins a steep, difficult, long trek to the summit. Tall spruce had displaced the hardwoods. The path became a series of wet and slippery exposed rock ledges. Looking ahead, we saw more of the same. The graveled surface of the trail made for difficult footing. If you have small children, you'll have to help them along.

The Summit of Owl's Head. After a half-hour along this steep section, the end was near. The summit is reached by a series of short, very difficult, switchbacks. By now you may regret having started this climb, but when you reach the summit and continue past it a short distance to the ledges just south, you'll find the view no less than spectacular. The entire Presidential Range can be seen to the east.

The northern peaks, as well as Mounts Washington and Monroe, were covered by clouds the day we climbed. However, the southern peaks from Eisenhower to Webster were clearly visible. There was an excellent view of Crawford Notch. Mount Willard is the low, flat mountain at the head of the notch. The Willey Range rises steeply to its right and Webster rises to its left. Chocorua was visible 29 miles to the southeast. The panorama continues to the east and north.

To the south lies Cherry Mountain with its clearly visible tower. Martha's Mile, a trail of approximately one mile, leads to its summit. None in our group had the energy to hike Cherry, but we suspect this is also a fine mountain to climb.

The wind started blowing in strong gusts. We packed quickly and left. The first half-hour of our descent was very difficult. The trail is steep and especially slippery. Go slowly and avoid the damp rocks wherever possible. I went down with our younger child, and it wasn't clear who was helping whom. After the trail takes a sharp turn left, the descent becomes much easier and, consequently, more enjoyable. We were down in a little over an hour.

Go east on NH 115 to see where you've been. There's a fine view of Owl's Head.

This hike is long and very difficult. The view, however,

OWL'S HEAD

is so superb that the effort is worth it. Go on a clear day, for the exertion is wasted if you get to the summit and can't see your feet. I wouldn't try this hike with children under four—you may get them up but getting them down will be most difficult.

Owl's Head

KEARSARGE NORTH

General Trail Description

This hike is along the Kearsarge North Trail to the open ledges extending from 2100 to 2300 feet in elevation on Kearsarge North. Descent is by the same route.

Trail Statistics

Starting Elevation	700'
Maximum Elevation	2300'
Total Vertical	1600'
Total Distance	4 Miles
Blazes	Yellow Paint on Ledges
Water	No

Our Experience

Difficulty	Moderate	
Our Pace	Slow	
Enjoyment	Good	
Time and Distance	Hours	Miles
To the Ledges	1:50	2
From the Ledges	1:10	2
Total	3:00	4

Directions to the Trail

Hurricane Mountain Road junctions with NH 16, 1.9 miles north of the Gulf station in North Conway. The trail leaves the north side of Hurricane Mountain Road, 1.5 miles east of its junction with NH 16. The sign marking the start of the trail had been stolen when we climbed in July, 1977, but the sign post was still there and the trail was quite obvious.

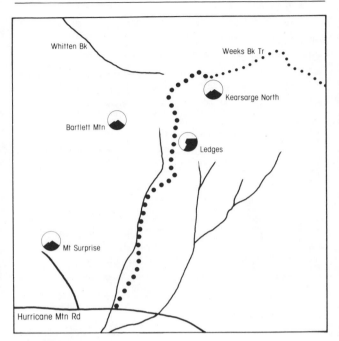

KEARSARGE NORTH

KEARSARGE NORTH

Kearsarge North is a familiar peak to those from the North Conway area. It rises as the highest mountain in a range running generally north-south from Bartlett to Conway. It was formerly called Pequawket after a tribe of Indians who once lived in the valleys of Conway and Fryeburg, Maine. An abandoned fire tower on the summit can be seen from the valley, making Kearsarge North an easily identifiable peak.

A series of open ledges on Kearsarge extend at elevations ranging from 2100 to 2300 feet. The two-mile climb to the ledges is a very pleasant hike.

The parking area for the Mount Kearsarge North Trail lies on the north side of Hurricane Mountain Road, 1.5 miles east of its junction with NH 16. The day we climbed the sign for the trail was missing from the post at the start. We assume it was removed by vandals. Signs are now often placed a ways in along the footpaths, removing them from the road in order to curb such destructive activities.

The trail begins as a wide path through a young woods. The first half-mile is level, traveling generally straight through a forest of aspen, maple, and birch. The trail begins a steeper ascent upon entering the White Mountain National Forest (indicated by a sign to the right of the trail). The moderate ascent is continual from this point to the ledges. We maintained a slow, steady pace that made the going quite easy.

Within 40 minutes, we came to a forest of huge hemlocks. Their small cones covered the path. Climbing a bit more steeply, we reached a sign for a spring with a side path right. We found the spring dry, so don't count on water here.

Pines and spruce had displaced the hemlocks at this elevation. The area was covered with blueberry bushes. When we hiked at the end of July, the berries were perfect for picking. Control your young ones from trampling through the bushes, since blueberries are much more appealing without footprints on them.

The Ledges. Continuing straight ahead, the trail leads to the first of a series of rocky, open ledges. Yellow paint on the rocks and small cairns mark the trail up the rock shelves. We had hiked an hour and a half.

Continuing up the ledges, a panorama opens up beneath you. The Ledges of Cathedral and White Horse, so imposing from the edge of Echo Lake in North Conway, appear insignificant below. The entire range of the Moat Mountains was clearly visible. This range forms the western wall of the valley from North Conway south to Conway. NH 16 meanders south through Mount Washington Valley. The bare face of Hurricane Mountain, at about the same altitude as the ledges, is near to the southeast.

Continuing up the bare rocks, we stopped where the trail again enters the woods. This spot provides the best views and is an ideal place for picnicking. We had been on the trail a little less than two hours. If you have small children, this is a convenient end to your hike.

The Summit of Kearsarge North. For those who wish to continue, you'll find the 50-minute climb to the summit of Kearsarge North well worth the effort. The AMC Guide states, "The view from the summit is one of the best in the mountains." It is. From the tower there is a sweeping, 360 degree view—Carter Notch, Pinkham Notch, Crawford Notch, the peaks surrounding Waterville Valley, Mounts Passaconaway and Chocorua.

Meet your party back on the ledges. The descent from here can be done in a little over an hour.

This is a fine hike with easy vertical. There is a natural stopping point on the ledges, while those who wish to continue can climb to the summit.

CASCADE PATH

General Trail Description

This trail is along the Cascade Path to the waterfalls on Cascade Brook. Following the path two-thirds of the distance in reverse, the Elephant Rock Trail is climbed to the Greeley Ledge Trail. The Greeley Ledge Trail is taken to where it comes out on one of the Snows Mountain ski slopes, very close to the hike's original starting point.

Trail Statistics

Starting Elevation	1600'
Maximum Elevation	2400'
Total Vertical	1000'
Total Distance	4 Miles
Blazes	Red on Cascade Path
	Yellow on Elephant Rock
	and Greeley Ledge Trails
Water	Yes

Our Experience

Difficulty	Easy
Our Pace	Slow
Enjoyment	Good

Time and Distance	Hours	Miles
Cascade Path to Falls	1:15	1.5
Falls to Elephant Rock Tr	:50	1.0
To Greeley Ledge Tr Return	1:10	1.5
Total	3:15	4.0

Directions to the Trail

Take Mad River Road, NH 49, into Waterville Valley. Keep bearing right passing by the clay tennis courts of the Laver-Emerson Tennis Camp (bring lots of money if you intend to enroll). The road ends at a parking area for the Finish Line Restaurant on your right. Park there. Walk across the end of a Snows Mountain ski slope toward the tennis courts. The trail, marked by a sign, begins just east of the courts.

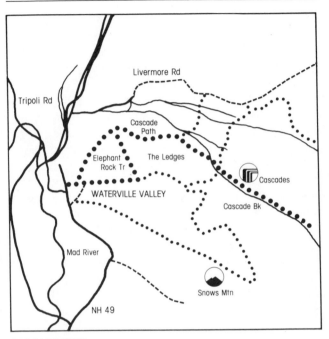

CASCADE PATH

CASCADE PATH

Waterville Valley. The town of Waterville Valley, incorporated in 1829, is surrounded by mountains approximately 4000 feet in elevation—Tecumseh, Osceola, Kancamagus, and Tripyramid. There are many footpaths within the area, both short and long. We found the Cascade Path to the falls on Cascade Brook very pleasant. If you're staying within the valley, plan to hike some of the many other trails.

We entered Waterville Valley along Tripoli Road. Just before its intersection with Mad River Road, NH 49, we came to an all-purpose gas station, post office, and general store. Here you can get a map of the hiking trails within the valley. They are kept under the counter (instead of dirty magazines) and cost an inflation-inflated, intolerable one buck!

We climbed Cascade Path on a perfect day that had begun with mist and dark clouds. Eventually the sky cleared, and the temperature rose to the lower 70's. A good breeze kept the bugs at bay.

The trail to the cascades is well-blazed in red and marked by frequent signs. Shortly after its start, the trail comes out on a dirt road. It turns left, past the Fire Warden's home, and crosses a ski slope before entering the woods again.

Small hemlocks line the path. A jeep road crosses just before a junction right with the Elephant Rock Trail. This junction marks the one-third point (0.5 mile). Tell the children who will be anxious to reach the falls how much further they must walk.

The woods were quiet and peaceful. We followed a narrow path through a forest of small, slim-trunked trees. Eventually, we crossed three log bridges in succession and reached the junction for Norway Rapids, marking the two-thirds point (1 mile). Stay right and follow the Cascade Brook to the lower falls.

The Cascades. The falls are a perfect goal for children. We climbed them on the right, passing cascade after cascade. We lost count, but there must be six or seven falls in succession, the longest drop being about 30 feet. When you sight a log shelter on your right, you've reached the top of the falls. We crossed over the rocks above the last cascade to the other side. Follow a trail down on this side and picnic anywhere along the many rock shelves of the falls.

While enjoying lunch on the rocks, I returned to the rushing stream to get water. I slipped and landed sitting in the brook. Soaked from waist to foot, I can hardly describe this hike because of my damp, blue-bleeding notebook. So . . . be careful at all times on wet rocks.

Elephant Rock Trail. We began our trek back and found more vertical returning than coming. At the junction with the Elephant Rock Trail, we decided to take it and return via a loop. The trail leaves left and comes immediately to Elephant Rock. A huge boulder hugs a dead tree trunk that is the "elephant's trunk".

The less-traveled path climbs easily through the woods and comes out on the ski slope we had crossed at the start of this hike. There was a fine view of the west peak of Mount Osceola from here. Climb to the top of the slope to view both Mount Osceola and Mount Tecumseh fencing the valley.

Greeley Ledge Trail. At the top of the ski slope we located the Greeley Ledge Trail. It enters the woods, descends what seemed a long distance, and comes out a short way down the ski trail. Perhaps it's better than walking down the slope? We ended our hike by walking the final hundred yards down the ski trail to the parking area.

The Cascade Path is a good introduction to hiking. The vertical is very easy with level stretches predominating. The cascades are a lovely climax to the hike. The loop over Elephant Rock Trail and Greeley Ledge Trail was marginal. Save yourselves the effort of trail-searching by returning the way you came.

HALL'S LEDGE

General Trail Description

The highest point and destination of this hike is Hall's Ledge, elevation 2600 feet. The hike is along Hall's Ledge Trail with a return over the same path.

Trail Statistics

Starting Elevation	1200'
Maximum Elevation	2600'
Total Vertical	1400'
Total Distance	3 Miles
Blazes	Oblong Cuts in Trees
	Small Cairns on the Trail
Water	Yes

Our Experience

Difficulty	Moderate	
Our Pace	Slow	
Enjoyment	Fair	
Time and Distance	Hours	Miles
NH 16 to the Clearing	2:00	1.5
Clearing to NH 16	1:30	1.5
Total	3:30	3.0

Directions to the Trail

The trail begins along NH 16, 5 miles north of the covered bridge in Jackson and 4.6 miles south of the AMC Pinkham Notch Camp. The trail lies directly opposite Dana Place on the east side of the highway.

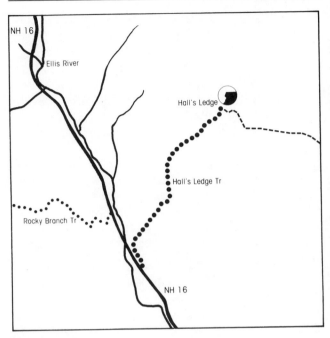

HALL'S LEDGE

HALL'S LEDGE

Hall's Ledge Trail is maintained by Dana Place, a country inn north of Jackson. In truth, it's not well-maintained. The trail is poorly marked, and the side trails that supposedly exist to the cascades and the ledge are not marked at all.

We climbed this trail late in June on a warm, muggy, partly cloudy day with temperatures in the 80's. There was virtually no wind, giving the mosquitoes a Thanksgiving.

The trail leaves the east side of NH 16 and begins a level stretch through the woods. Since it had rained for 24 hours before we climbed, the path was very wet. Apply repellent before you start. We didn't and were sorry as we applied it in the woods to the tune of sucking mosquitoes. The bugs were pesty and especially enjoyed young flesh.

The Brook. The path travels through a young forest of tall, thin birches. Within five minutes we crossed a small brook on two slippery logs, one almost completely decayed. We approached another brook rushing noisily over the rocks to our right. Get water at this stream, since the trail quickly ascends above the brook and there are no more opportunities.

The trail begins a moderate climb up the left bank of the brook, reaching a height of about 100 feet above the water where there is a distant view of the rushing cascades. There's supposedly a way to take a side path right to the falls, but we didn't see it during either our ascent or descent.

The seldom-traveled path eventually veers left from the brook and begins a difficult ascent. The path was steep and muddy. Don't expect many markings—small cairns dot the trail but are hard to locate. Blazes cut in the trees are few and far between. We found the descent of this section especially hard to follow and had to backtrack a number of times to find our way.

This steep rise took us half an hour. Coaxing was necessary to keep small legs moving.

Once you've made this steep ascent, it's easy going. The path turns right and passes through a lovely, mature forest. Huge maples suffuse the land. If you look carefully, you'll see an occasional oak. Beeches are abundant, and older birches rise a hundred feet from the forest floor. The woods slowly change from hardwoods to spruce and fir. Walking along this path covered with soft spruce needles, we found fewer bugs and easier climbing.

Near a clearing, the children saw a small, gray snake. Being basically a coward, I was unable to snare it for them.

A Clearing. We came to a logging road with a clearing to our left and views to the northwest. Through the haze, we could see Mount Washington, Boot Spur, and the Gulf of Slides. We backtracked to find the supposed-trail off the main path to Hall's Ledge but were unsuccessful.

We returned to the clearing for lunch. The bugs were a bit unpleasant. Clouds rolled in, engulfing the summit of Mount Washington as we ate. We left shortly, our younger child enjoying the descent much more than she had the upward climb.

This hike has some fine features—the woods after the steep ascent and the spruce forest. However, the obscure trail and the lack of a discernible ledge as a goal made this hike less enjoyable for us than many of our other hikes.

FRANKENSTEIN CLIFF

General Trail Description

This hike is along the Frankenstein Cliff Trail to its junction with the Arethusa-Ripley Falls Trail. The Arethusa-Ripley Falls Trail is taken to Ripley Falls and its northern end near the Willey House Railroad Station.

Trail Statistics

Starting Elevation	1200'
Maximum Elevation	2560'
Total Vertical	1360'
Total Distance	3.5 Miles
Blazes (sporadic)	Yellow at Start of Frankenstein Cliff Trail; Blue where Cliff Trail Ends
Water	Frankenstein — No Ripley — Yes

Our Experience

Difficulty	Difficult
Our Pace	Slow
Enjoyment	Good

Time and Distance	Hours	Miles
US 302 to Cliff	1:20	.9
Cliff to A-R Falls Tr	:55	1.0
A-R Falls Tr to Ripley Falls	:55	1.1
Ripley Falls to Willey Station	:30	.5
Total	3:40	3.5

Directions to the Trail

The trail leaves US 302, 8.6 miles north of the Bartlett Hotel and just south of the Dry River Campground near a bridge crossing the Saco River. There is no convenient parking, so park along the shoulder of the road. The trail is unmarked but leaves the highway on the west side of the road, immediately across from the south end of the bridge. Look for an obvious path into the woods.

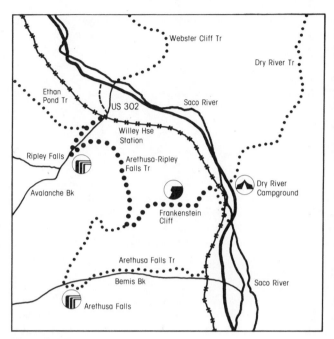

FRANKENSTEIN CLIFF

FRANKENSTEIN CLIFF

Contrary to more romantic notions, Frankenstein Cliff is named after George L. Frankenstein, an artist from Cincinnati who painted scenes of the White Mountains.

The sheer face of Frankenstein Cliff is a stark landmark along US 302 when driving north through Crawford Notch. The Frankenstein Cliff Trail to the outlook above the cliff is decidedly difficult, especially for young children. If you plan to do this hike, prepare yourselves for a tough haul. If you take young ones, be ready to give them plenty of help.

We climbed on a perfect day. The temperatures were in the upper 60's to lower 70's. There were virtually no clouds. The sky was a deep blue, a color seldom seen during the summer months in the mountains. Our views of Mount Washington were totally unobscured.

Locating the Trail. Our first difficulty was finding the trail. Recent widening of US 302 near the trail's start must have caused the demise of the New Hampshire Division of Parks trail sign. Near the south end of a newly constructed bridge crossing the Saco River, we entered the woods on what was clearly a trail. The path immediately came to a T where we turned right. The trail parallels US 302 for a short distance and then turns left, uphill, on a path marked by yellow blazes. We reached a sign for the Frankenstein Cutoff and the Frankenstein Cliff Trail. We had come 0.3 mile according to the trail sign, but it didn't seem that far. You'll especially think this stretch was short in contrast to the next 0.6 mile!

The Frankenstein Cliff Trail continues uphill and travels under the Frankenstein Trestle. The fun begins as the path starts a series of switchbacks up the steep slope. It's easy to start up the remains of an old slide, but you'll soon discover your error and remain on the switchbacks. Initially, the trail zig-zags to the left of the slide, but it soon crosses the slide and continues its winding course to the right. The trail was especially tough because of its narrowness, only one-person wide in many places, and its slippery, rocky composition. The path was covered with the remnants of decayed rock, a surface we have learned to respect.

After about an hour, we came face to face with a sheer rock cliff, mountain ash sprouting from its crevices. The trail appeared to go around the cliff in both directions; we went right and had no difficulty.

The hardwood forest gives way to spruce and fir. The needle-carpeted path soon leads through a spruce-lined avenue to the outlook above the cliff.

Frankenstein Cliff. The outlook, covered with red pines, gives fine views south. The mountain with the rocky summit to the east is Mount Crawford. Just to the west is Mount Bemis with Mount Nancy rising to the southwest. Near to the southwest look carefully and you'll see an open, rocky patch in the forest. It's the bed of Arethusa Falls on the Bemis Brook. These falls are the highest in New Hampshire, over 200 feet from the top to the pool below. The marked contrast in the woods, starting at the falls and continuing east to the highway, outlines the path of the Bemis Brook as it flows to the Saco River. Fifteen miles to the south, poking its head up between Mountains Bear and Tremont, lies Mount Chocorua.

The trail continues, unfortunately, up. Our children thought they had done their vertical penance for the day and were unhappy about the additional climbing. However, the forest was pleasant and, within 20 minutes, the trail passed the 2451 foot summit to the south. It shortly attains its maximum elevation of 2560 feet and begins an easy, gradual downgrade to its junction with the Arethusa-Ripley Falls Trail.

The Arethusa-Ripley Falls Trail. Going left to Arethusa Falls or right to Ripley Falls, the distances are the same—1.1 miles. However, Ripley Falls are much closer to US 302 and, therefore, make for a shorter hike. Also, Arethusa Falls is much more popular and may not give you the privacy you seek.

We turned right. The woods gradually change from evergreens to broadleafed birches and maples. The trail was deserted. After 50 minutes, we heard the rushing water of Ripley Falls. We approached the cascades on our left. As we neared their head, we took a side path left and climbed onto the rocks between the upper and lower falls.

FRANKENSTEIN CLIFF

Ripley Falls. The upper falls are short, while the lower falls drop about 100 feet. Be careful on the rocks so you don't drop that same 100 feet. Shallow pools had formed on the rocks between the falls. They were ideal for wading. Our children thoroughly enjoyed themselves and, in this moment of weakness, said the climb was worth the effort.

We descended to the bottom of the falls along short switchbacks. We crossed the Avalanche Brook and continued our return on the other side. The path travels the north bank of the brook, high above its rushing waters. In 0.4 mile, we met the junction with the Ethan Pond Trail.

Between this junction and the RR tracks look for an outlook to your left giving fine views of Mount Webster and Mount Willard with its sheer rock face. At the RR crossing turn right, go about 20 feet, and take a path that leads to a parking area. We followed the dirt road from this parking area to US 302, two miles north of where we had parked our car. I hitchhiked back with some fine people who sensed I was exhausted.

Including our stops, we were on the trail for over five hours. Our younger child would have preferred a shorter climb, but her energy quickly renewed leaving me wishing she had hiked longer.

This is a long and difficult hike. If you have older children they will love it. The steep ascent gave our son a feeling of accomplishment and superiority as he left his panting parents behind. After reaching the outlook above the cliff, you can return along the same path. This will make for a shorter hike, but the descent will require caution. For another shorter, easier hike, take the Arethusa-Ripley Falls Trail from the Willey Station to Ripley Falls and back. The falls are superb.

Upper Pools of Ripley Falls

MOUNT HEDGEHOG

General Trail Description

The U.N.H. trail is a loop around Mount Hedgehog. The mountain can be climbed either from the east (3 miles) or from the west (2 miles). We chose to climb the mountain from the west and descend around the east.

Trail Statistics

Starting Elevation	1250'
Maximum Elevation	2520'
Total Vertical	1270'
Total Distance	5 Miles
Blazes	Blue on Trees
	Yellow on Ledges
Water	No

Our Experience

Difficulty	Moderate
Our Pace	Moderate
Enjoyment	Very Good

Time and Distance	Hours	Miles
NH 112 to Allen's Ledge	:45	1
Allen's Ledge to Summit	:55	1
Summit to East Ledges	:45	1
East Ledges to NH 112	1:30	2
Total	3:55	5

Directions to the Trail

The trail leaves the south side of the Kancamagus Highway, NH 112, 1.8 miles west of its junction with Bear Notch Road and 0.2 mile east of the White Mountain National Forest Passaconaway Campground. Park your car on the shoulder of the road near the trail's entrance. The trail is indicated by a sign marked U.N.H. TRAIL.

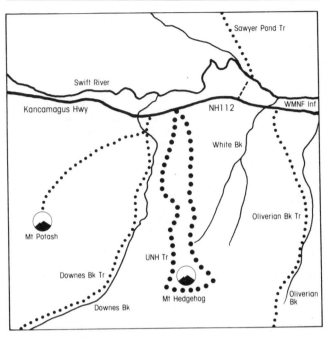

MOUNT HEDGEHOG

MOUNT HEDGEHOG

Mount Hedgehog lies north of the looming mass of Mount Passaconaway. A loop trail provides varied outlooks along the mountain's length. Once you conquer the summit and all the ledges, you will have had views in every direction.

Plan a full day for this hike, since you will walk over five miles and climb almost 1300 feet of vertical. This is a decidedly long hike for small children. Fortunately, the day we climbed our young ones gave us no trouble.

We hiked in good weather. The lower-70's temperature was ideal for climbing. There was a slight breeze and light, wispy clouds in the sky.

The trail begins along a grass-covered road that diverges within five minutes from the highway. The left, less-used-looking path leads to the trail that ascends the mountain via the east side, while the right, more-traveled-looking path, is the trail around the west side. We chose the right branch to climb and were happy with our selection. The summit is reached more quickly, in two miles versus three, a fine ledge marks the half-way point in distance, and we found the trail more pleasant than the eastern return path.

The wide road right leads through an area of large pines and spruce. Just after crossing an intersecting road, the path narrows. To our right was a large area devastated by logging. The woods we traveled through must also have been recently logged, since the hardwoods were young and thin. Stumps of former giants lined the trail.

The trail begins a moderate rise, skirts a clearing to the right, and veers away to the left. We approached a magnificent area of tall hemlocks.

A half-hour out, we turned sharply left at a sign with an arrow nailed to a tree. The moderate ascent continues through the hemlock forest. Trees rise 60 feet above the rock-strewn forest floor.

Allen's Ledge After 45 minutes, we came to Allen's Ledge. Both the ledge trail and main path were clearly marked by signs on a tree. The trail straight leads to the ledge, while the main path turns right.

The ledge gives excellent views north. The many-peaked ridge of Bear Mountain was very close. Mount

Washington was visible beyond the valley between Bear and Tremont Mountains. To the east was the long ridge of the Moat Mountains.

We left the ledge and continued our climb. The moderately-graded trail travels through a forest of tall spruce. The path's soft cushion of needles made for easy treading. The woods were alive with seedlings, starting their struggle to survive.

Thirty-five minutes from Allen's Ledge, we came to a fine outlook through the trees. The massive mountain to the northwest is Carrigain. Look carefully and you'll note a small dot on the summit. It's a tower. The long slope of Signal Ridge trails off Carrigain to your right. The mountain with the sheer side cliffs is Webster, rising to form the eastern wall of Crawford Notch some 17 miles away.

The Summit of Hedgehog. The ascent becomes fairly steep, but the trail is unobstructed. It's merely a matter of pushing forward to a level stretch just before the summit. The summit is marked by a yellow circle painted on the rock ledge. You can find ledges to the right giving views north and west and ledges to the left giving views south and east.

To the south, the closest, largest mountain is Passaconaway. Mount Chocorua is seen to the east. Far to the northwest, a small tower visible on the summit, is Cannon Mountain. Cannon, also known as Profile Mountain, is famous for its rock profile Great Stone Face.

The summit of Hedgehog is a fine place to rest and congratulate yourselves on a successful conquest. From the ledge looking east, the East Ledges can be seen below. They look very close, and, truly, are only about 200 feet below the summit. However, it took us almost an hour to reach them on our descent.

The East Trail. The trail down follows yellow blazes on the rocks. It heads generally west, zig-zagging down around the rocky sides of the summit ledges. This westerly direction gives way, by short turns and jogs, until you're heading in the right direction—east. The trail passes through the remains of a former slide where huge boulders rest, stilled from their once short but violent free-fall. Many of the rocks with flat upper surfaces host

MOUNT HEDGEHOG

gardens of vegetation, ferns, moss, and seedlings, as the process of stone decay begins its long, silent course.

The East Ledges. Forty-five minutes after leaving the summit, we reached the East Ledges. Following along the easterly edge of the ledge, we found a barely legible sign with an arrow pointing right. Moving onto more rocky precipices, we eventually found a sign marked PATH that signaled an entrance into the woods. A short way down this trail, through an outlook in the trees, we came to our last views of the day. There was a fine view of Crawford Notch, marked by the sheer face of Mount Webster to the east and the slide-scarred face of Mount Willey to the west. We had our last glimpse of Mount Washington.

A half-hour from the East Ledges, we crossed a small stream. This was the only water we encountered the entire day, so fill your canteens before you begin.

The trail now travels through an older hardwood forest. Huge beeches and maples fill the woods. The trail was rough with roots, rocks, and rubble, making the descent difficult. The contrast in trail composition between the nearly adjacent west and east trails was surprising.

About two miles from the summit, we traveled through a cool, shady, pleasant area of hemlocks. Fighting exhaustion, we were anxious for the hike to end. We reached the grassy road two hours after leaving the summit. By this time, the 15-minute walk to the junction with the main road seemed an eternity. The feisty mosquitoes prodded us into moving on quickly.

Five hours from the time of our departure we were back to the Kancamagus Highway.

This is a good, solid hike in the mountains. It's a wonderful trail through the woods, and the many, varied views are sheer pleasure. If you have no trouble with this one, your family is ready for the 4000-footers.

UNH Trail to Hedgehog

HIKES BY MAXIMUM ELEVATION

HIKES BY TIME